"Gary Burge's aptly chose. that the New Testament is not just a book full of doctrines, promises, or ethics, but has to be understood within the overarching grand narrative of the Bible as a whole, from creation to new creation. Within that framework he helps us understand the cultural and religious context into which God entered in Jesus of Nazareth, the starkly surprising and challenging nature of 'the good news' that Jesus and his apostles preached, and the glorious future that God's mission will accomplish for the whole creation. However well you think you know your New Testament, this will help you see it through fresh eyes and gain many new insights in the process."

Christopher J. H. Wright, author of *The Old Testament in Seven Sentences*

"Burge wakes up his readers to the provocation that is the gospel of Jesus Christ. That which many modern readers assume as commonplace (i.e., Jesus came to die on a cross for my sins), shocked the beliefs and lives of the first Christians. With rootedness in history and careful attention to the beauty of the text, Burge invites readers to do the hard—and very good—work of understanding the overarching message of the Christian faith."

Amy Peeler, associate professor of New Testament, Wheaton College, associate rector, St. Mark's Episcopal Church, Geneva, IL

"Burge gives us a panoramic vision of some of the major themes in the Scriptures in this wonderfully accessible book. Sometimes we plunge into reading the Scriptures without an understanding of its larger story line, and we all know that it is difficult to understand the parts of a story without having a grasp of the whole picture. Burge unpacks the meaning of the Messiah, cross, Spirit, and new creation, along with other central themes. This book is a great tool for personal reading, for group studies, and for preachers and students."

Thomas Schreiner, associate dean and James Buchanan Harrison Professor of New Testament Interpretation at The Southern Baptist Theological Seminary

"To sum up the New Testament in seven sentences seems a daunting task. Gary Burge succeeds in doing so by engaging its story. He draws on seven central New Testament statements to retell the story of God's work in Christ. In the process, he widens the lens to show how the entire biblical story culminates in Jesus' person and work. It is an accessible and inviting book!"

Jeannine Brown, professor of New Testament and director of online programs, Bethel Seminary

"Gary Burge is the best of communicators. He lays out the central message of the New Testament with such clarity and insight that those who read this work will close the cover and wonder why they had not heard the gospel this way before. Burge makes the best of New Testament studies accessible while never talking down as he brings each reader up to understand the depths of God's wonder-filled work in Christ. Read, reflect, and rejoice!"

Gene L. Green, professor emeritus of New Testament, Wheaton College

THE NEW TESTAMENT

IN SEVEN SENTENCES

A SMALL INTRODUCTION TO A VAST TOPIC

GARY M. BURGE

ivp
Academic
An imprint of InterVarsity Press
Downers Grove, Illinois

InterVarsity Press
P.O. Box 1400, Downers Grove, IL 60515-1426
ivpress.com
email@ivpress.com

InterVarsity Press® is the book-publishing division of InterVarsity Christian Fellowship/USA®, a movement of students and faculty active on campus at hundreds of universities, colleges, and schools of nursing in the United States of America, and a member movement of the International Fellowship of Evangelical Students. For information about local and regional activities, visit intervarsity.org.

Figures 8.1 and 8.2: Rembrandt van Rijn, Christ Preaching (The Hundred Guilder Print), *circa 1646-1650 / Wikimedia Commons*

Cover design: Bradley Joiner
Interior design: Beth McGill

ISBN 978-0-8308-5476-9 (print)
ISBN 978-0-8308-5645-9 (digital)

Printed in the United States of America ∞

Library of Congress Cataloging-in-Publication Data
Names: Burge, Gary M., 1952- author.
Title: The New Testament in seven sentences : a small introduction to a vast topic / Gary M. Burge.
Description: Downers Grove, Illinois : IVP Academic, an imprint of InterVarsity Press, [2019] |
    Includes bibliographical references and index.
Identifiers: LCCN 2019027282 (print) | LCCN 2019027283 (ebook) | ISBN 9780830854769
    (paperback) | ISBN 9780830856459 (ebook)
Subjects: LCSH: Bible. New Testament—Introductions. | Bible. New Testament—Theology.
Classification: LCC BS2330.3 .B865 2019 (print) | LCC BS2330.3 (ebook) | DDC 225.6/1—dc23
LC record available at https://lccn.loc.gov/2019027282
LC ebook record available at https://lccn.loc.gov/2019027283

P 22 21 20 19 18 17 16 15 14 13 12 11 10 9 8 7 6 5 4 3 2 1
Y 39 38 37 36 35 34 33 32 31 30 29 28 27 26 25 24 23 22 21 20 19

To the Midweek Community

Willow Creek Community Church

South Barrington, Illinois

CONTENTS

INTRODUCTION

For over fifteen years I had the privilege of serving on the teaching roster at the midweek service of a large church in Chicago. The common denominator of those who came was simple: intentionality. They were earnest about their faith and wanted tools to grow. And they were sincere. Over the years, we taught through the Psalms, Daniel, Colossians, the Farewell of Jesus, James, and the Gospel of Mark. One season we even summarized the main themes of theology. And every week they came back wanting more.[1]

If I had a dream for those wonderful people—and for my many students over the years—it would be that something more was added to their learning. We often explore individual passages of Scripture without seeing the whole. The individual passage is inspiring and easy to grasp while explaining the whole is far more difficult. It takes patience. It is far easier to work through a short story in Mark's Gospel each week than it is to understand the grand sweep of his Gospel's message. The latter requires synthesizing and a comparison of one passage against another. There are thousands of Christians who could do this very thing if only they had the right tools to guide them. We are taught individual passages of the Bible or limited themes from theology, but no one is weaving together the whole tapestry.

The aim of this small book is to weave this larger tapestry. And if we do it well, then the parts of the story we love to study will suddenly take on newer meaning. Without the larger tapestry, we really cannot see the scope of what Jesus is doing in the New Testament. We gain glimpses of his activity (a miracle, a confrontation) or his teaching (a parable, a conversation), but without the larger picture, these things lose their significance. In fact, I would suggest that we *reduce* the importance of Jesus when we study each of his stories in isolation. He becomes someone who provides episodes of inspiration without the colossal impact that his story requires.

This is what we need for the New Testament. Another way to think about it is that we need an aerial view of the landscape. We study the valleys in detail, but we're not sure how they are connected to the whole. Only a view from thirty thousand feet will enable us to see it properly. A good map will do this as well. We refer to the Sea of Galilee regularly, but I've stood at its edge with students and adults and realized that they had never understood "where it was" or "what it was" until that moment. They had no mental map of the terrain. But they did have a good recollection of episodes that took place on this famous sea. (In fact, since we refer to it as a "sea" they first have to get used to the idea that it is a lake.) When we see something in its broader context, the part takes on a new meaning from the whole.

Consider this quote: Once, in the middle of Jesus' public ministry, Peter is asked by Jesus to identify him. Peter responds, "You are the Messiah, the Son of the living God." Then Jesus says, "Blessed are you, Simon son of Jonah, for this was not revealed to you by flesh and blood, but by my Father in heaven" (Matthew 16:16-17).

I am convinced it is difficult if not impossible for the average person to make sense of these two verses. Even though they are well known, they are filled with assumptions that most first-century

Christian readers would have understood—assumptions that are lost on us. For many today Peter's announcement simply means that Jesus is God's spectacular gift to us. Jesus is a messenger from God, a courier of good news. All of this is true, but there is far more assumed in these words than we think. This is what we need to probe.

At root is this: What is the profound announcement that the Gospels are making regarding Jesus? Do they think that Jesus is making a personal impact on those who encounter him, or do they see him as having an impact on the course of Israel's history? Or is it both? Perhaps they even see him as having an effect not just on Israel but on the world itself, a shifting on the eras, a new chapter in human history, an unexpected intervention by God in human history.

We are used to film sequels. Imagine a film or television series that is now in its fifth year (think Star Wars, Battlestar Galactica, Game of Thrones, or Downton Abbey). Imagine starting at the third season and trying to understand what's going on. It might be possible, but I doubt it. In Battlestar Galactica we'd never know that advanced robots called Cylons had rebelled against their makers (humans), destroyed the earth, and set out to defeat humans around the galaxy who are secretly living in twelve colonies. Now we've joined the story many years later aboard one rusty, old (and very cool) starship called Galactica, led by Commander William Adama (Edward James Olmos). This ship survived the Cylon attack because Adama is a Luddite who uses old-world technology (no network!) and the Cylons don't know how to infiltrate his command and defense systems. Adama even uses an old wired telephone in his office! And the Cylons are after him!

If the paragraph I just wrote sounds confusing, it has served its purpose. Imagine joining this story without its backstory. Nothing would make sense. What's a Cylon? Who is Adama?

What are the Twelve Colonies? What century is this? And why do all these crew members seem homeless? Episode three just doesn't tell us.

This is the fundamental problem we face in the books of the New Testament. They don't provide the backstory, and without it, many of their themes simply escape us. We believe that Jesus fulfills prophecy. But we don't fully know the prophetic expectation that was held closely during his time.

Our assignment, then, is to tell the backstory. It is an old story reaching back into the Old Testament but shaped particularly by the events two hundred years before Jesus. We will try to map the terrain and use as our guide seven sentences (representing themes) that are essential if we are to understand the New Testament. And while we will be forced to leave out a lot, still, we can map the major contours of thought, the big ideas, so that the shorter stories begin to make sense.

The challenge of a book such as this involves selecting which themes are essential to this fuller understanding. I begin with (1) fulfillment because basically the New Testament is arguing that the story of the Old Testament has come to completion in the arrival of Jesus-the-Messiah. The next chapter covers the central organizing idea of Jesus, namely (2) the kingdom. This was the fundamental project that Jesus was establishing, and we need to understand it. However, a part of his mission included (3) the cross, an unexpected and confusing feature of his mission. The cross not only established a new covenant but paved the way for a new, forgiven, and transformed community that the New Testament celebrates. The cross opens the way to understand God's generosity and (4) grace. No theme has been more central to Christians for two thousand years than grace, and yet we'll learn that it is taken for granted and often misunderstood. The outgrowth of this grand project of fulfillment and kingdom building is a new (5) covenant community. This refashions what it means to be God's people in the world who stand under the blessings that began with Abraham. This community celebrates a new life to be sure, but it also celebrates the gift of (6) the Spirit, which had been promised throughout the Old Testament. Finally, the New Testament describes the (7) completion of all things. The Scriptures view time as linear: it begins and it ends. And so the New Testament reminds us to look forward with anticipation to when God will complete all things and return creation to its intended purposes. These themes—fulfillment, kingdom, cross, grace, covenant, spirit, and completion—offer a theological rhythm that gives us a deep foundation to understand our faith.

Recently a friend at church told me that he wasn't interested in theology but rather wanted people to have good feelings— feelings that would help them through life and enjoy Jesus. I agreed to a point. But I also realize that we need more. Because feelings can sometimes be an unreliable guide to how our life in this world works. Understanding the deep structures of New Testament thought—to think the thoughts of Paul or Luke or John after them—may help us live lives of strength and resilience and celebration for what God has done in Christ.

The idea for this series belongs to Daniel Reid, the now-retired senior editor at InterVarsity Press. He imagined the series and recruited many of us to launch books that will do what this book does. Anna Moseley Gissing now works on the series at IVP, and to her belongs the credit for seeing the project to completion. Her insights and constructive comments have made this book far better than it would have been otherwise. Copyediting was done by Ashley Davila, and the layout and cover artists were Beth McGill and Bradley Joiner. Every book is a team effort, and as authors we know well that we rely on the wisdom of many to bring books like this to print.

one

FULFILLMENT

*Simon Peter answered, "You are the
Messiah, the Son of the living God."*

MATTHEW 16:16

E ach of the Gospel writers knew they were introducing a
story that had enormous significance. They were not
telling a story that might compare with the courageous or inspiring Jewish narratives that were well known in their day. Nor
were they profiling a heroic character who brought a message
to Israel but was rejected and martyred. They knew that they
were saying something more. Something epic. Something that
compared with the great stories of the Old Testament or perhaps
even the Roman world. As we'll see, this story was even a rival
to the great story of the Emperor Augustus (but more on that
later). Matthew wanted to write with an epic tone, so he imitated the style of Greek that they read regularly in their two-
hundred-year-old Greek translation of the Old Testament. He
was giving his story a "biblical" sound. It was like telling a religious story today and sounding like we just stepped out of the
King James Bible.

These Gospel writers believed that a colossal shift had taken place in Judaism—and in the world—and they are about to tell us what it is. And they knew it was going to be controversial. The Gospel writers do not shy away from the fact that whenever this story is told in full by Jesus, crowds are either won over or they are resistant and disturbed. It reminds me of Rabbi Jacob Neusner's popular book, *A Rabbi Talks with Jesus.*[1] Neusner describes how he would have respected much of what Jesus taught but that he also would have disagreed with Jesus profoundly. He would have rejected some of the more important things Jesus was saying. If Jesus is new wine and Israel is the wineskin, an old wineskin no less, Neusner takes offense that the arrival of Jesus will break the old wineskin (Luke 5:37). And Neusner is exactly right. Jesus is not just one more teacher; Jesus is *the* Teacher who had shifted everything. Something epic was happening, and for many teachers in Israel, Jesus was a stone that would make many stumble (Romans 9:32; 11:11; Luke 7:23).

Mark opens this epic with these words: "The beginning of the good news about Jesus the Messiah" (Mark 1:1). Some ancient Greek scribes even expanded on Mark's first verse in order to underscore its significance: "The beginning of the good news about Jesus the Messiah, *the Son of God.*" These words, "good news," "Messiah," even "Son of God," are so loaded with meaning it is difficult to underestimate them. But they all point to this same premise: something enormous has happened, and it is good, very good.

WHAT THE GOSPELS ARE DOING

But first let's be clear about what the Gospels are and what they are not. Despite the fact that the Gospels open the New Testament, they are not the oldest writings of the New Testament. The earliest Christians were not writing the story of Jesus during his lifetime. His closest followers (called apostles) followed ...... , carefully learned many of the things he taught, and imitated his way of life. But their most profound experience—the experience that truly converted them—was the resurrection. They understood that they were witnesses to something phenomenal (John 15:27; Acts 1:8; 2:32), and soon this exposure was coupled to an intense experience of the Holy Spirit that galvanized their faith and confirmed their commitment to be followers of Jesus even if they were abused, imprisoned, or killed. This was a story they could not walk away from. In other words, it was an experience, a transformative experience of Jesus in power that brought them to the faith that they had throughout their lives.

The life of Jesus certainly was compelling, but the resurrection of Jesus was profoundly confirming that God was at work here in ways they could barely measure. Notice the speeches of the book of Acts: when these early believers preach about Jesus, the resurrection is the critical element in every presentation. It is the power of Jesus that converts, not well-reasoned presentations about his public life.

The earliest writer to reflect on these things may have been Paul. We cannot be certain whether other letters in the New Testament (James?) came earlier, but it is in Paul, an early Jewish convert to Christ, that we hear the earliest explanations about what Jesus meant to Judaism and the world. For some scholars, Paul's letter to the Roman region of Galatia ("Galatians") is the earliest Christian document we own, and here we can see Paul formulating an explanation of Jesus that guided early believers who did not own a Gospel. But note carefully that in his letters we find virtually nothing about the earthly life of Jesus. No birth or baptism, no record of Jesus' miracles, nor even any specifics about the cross and resurrection. Paul announces Jesus' betrayal, death, and resurrection, but he doesn't point to the details of the story about it.

At some point the community of Christians recognized that if their faith was anchored to the resurrected, living Jesus, they wanted to know more about him. If it was Jesus in power who was transforming the world, then it made sense that reflection on his earthly life was necessary as well. The resurrection forced the early church to rethink the meaning of what they had seen during Jesus' earthly life.

Throughout the Gospels much of Jesus' teaching and activity seemed incomprehensible to his followers. When he told a parable, they struggled to comprehend it (Mark 4:13). When he fed the five thousand, they simply couldn't understand its deeper meaning (Mark 6:52). They found the cross to be completely beyond their ability to take in (Mark 8:32-33; 9:32). But after Jesus died, after he had been raised from the dead and the Spirit awakened their minds to what was really happening, everything became clear.

The story of the disciples on the Emmaus road illustrates this. On Easter Sunday Jesus encounters two people who believed in him, and yet the cross had dashed their hopes. They knew about the cross and had heard rumors about an empty tomb. But these men hadn't seen the resurrected Jesus themselves. They were discouraged. Then Jesus—unrecognized at this point—began to explain everything to them. "He said, 'How foolish you are, and how slow to believe all that the prophets have spoken! Did not the Messiah have to suffer these things and then enter his glory?' And beginning with Moses and all the Prophets, he explained to them what was said in all the Scriptures concerning himself" (Luke 24:25-27). However, the men still didn't recognize Jesus. But they stopped to eat in a village, and when Jesus broke bread and prayed in his customary way, suddenly it happened—"then their eyes were opened and they recognized him" (Luke 24:31). Notice that the resurrected Jesus explains his true identity and opens their minds to comprehend it.

John's Gospel makes this experience explicit. ˈ
could not understand the cleansing of the temple
drove out the money-changers. It was his resurrection that en-
abled them to remember and interpret what Jesus meant in his
public life. "After he was raised from the dead, his disciples recalled what he had said. Then they believed the scripture and the
words that Jesus had spoken" (John 2:22). Likewise, John tells us
that the disciples barely understood Jesus' triumphal entry into
Jerusalem (John 12:16). Then John says, "At first his disciples did
not understand all this. Only after Jesus was glorified did they
realize that these things had been written about him and that
these things had been done to him" (John 12:16). It was the resurrection that prompted research and reflection on Jesus' earthly
life, and this effort would be guided by the work of the Holy
Spirit (John 14:26). Note again the twin points of early Christian
thinking: resurrection and Spirit. Both together led the church
to revisit and comprehend Jesus' preresurrection life.

This investigation into Jesus' life resulted in the collection and
preservation of Jesus' story. We think of the leadership of the
earliest community as the custodians of "the Jesus Tradition." In
the Gospels, they are called "apostles." Sometimes they are called
"The Twelve." They were committed to the archive of stories that
circulated from Jesus' life. Were Jesus' sayings collated and collected? Were many memorized? Were they circulating in oral
form? Were written memoranda kept? A wide number of
scholars would affirm each of these.

But the great task before them was not only the important
custodial work of preserving and passing on what Jesus had
taught and done. The great task was writing an *explanatory narrative* that organized and interpreted what all of this meant. And
this is when we come to the Gospels themselves. Their authors'
aim was to put some form to the meaning of Jesus' life from the

very beginning. The collection of materials at their disposal may have been far larger than what we see today in the New Testament. But in their selection and ordering of events from Jesus' life, they were painting a portrait of him using the building materials of the "Jesus Tradition" that had been preserved within the community. Think of this as an artist who is building a two-hour film on a complex set of stories—perhaps a war or a person's life. When the artist selects one story over another, or chooses an arrangement of these stories, it all contributes to the final picture we get to watch.

Now here is a key: the Gospel writers were not just compilers stringing together a long list of events from Jesus. They were theologians, or perhaps artists, writing up the story so that it made interpretive sense to anyone who would read it. Jesus had to be explained for audiences in later generations who had never heard him. And while that first generation was still living, they could serve as eyewitnesses for what everyone knew to be true about Jesus.

THE FIRST PRIMARY IDEA

When Peter refers to Jesus as "the Messiah" or when Mark opens his Gospel with a reference to Jesus Christ as the Messiah, we quickly uncover one of the central claims of the New Testament. *Messiah* is a Hebrew word that simply means someone who is anointed. It is translated into Greek as "Christos" or in English "Christ." Anointing is simply putting something (such as oil) on something else (such as someone's head). Anointing could be ceremonial, such as when David is anointed the king of Israel (1 Samuel 16:13). Or it could be a social courtesy, such as when guests are greeted at a dinner party (Luke 7:46). In ceremonial anointing for kings (1 Samuel 16:12-13), priests (Exodus 29:7), or prophets (1 Kings 19:16), the anointing is symbolic of God's

Spirit, who is empowering the work of the person and confirming their role. When that anointing is jeopardized through misconduct, such as David's sin with Bathsheba, then this risks the removal of God's Spirit (Psalm 51:11).

Therefore, the first fundamental affirmation of the New Testament is that Jesus is an "anointed one," bearing God's Spirit. "Christ" (*Christos*) is used almost five hundred times in the New Testament to describe Jesus. It is the central affirmation of every Christian confession from the beginning. Following Peter's sermon at Pentecost—the first Christian sermon—the crowd wonders what they should do. Peter says, "Repent and be baptized, every one of you, in the name of Jesus Christ for the forgiveness of your sins. And you will receive the gift of the Holy Spirit" (Acts 2:38). Belief is centered on "Jesus Christ," or perhaps, Jesus the anointed one. Jesus Christ is not Jesus' full name. It is an affirmation of belief. Jesus is the Messiah.

But what about the backstory to this name? The New Testament is not claiming that Jesus is simply one more anointed figure in Israel's history. He is not "a messiah." He is *the* Messiah. And this takes more explanation.

THE PROBLEM AND THE SOLUTION

When I was a student I was once on a Swiss train traveling from Geneva to Zurich. I was traveling alone for the day, and an older Jewish rabbi sat next to me. He immediately struck up a conversation. And after I disclosed that I had been studying in the Middle East for a year and was on my way home in a roundabout way, he enquired more about my personal studies. I told him that I had worked in both political science and religion and was interested in how these interfaced in the thorny world of the Middle East. And I said I was a Christian. Immediately he lit up. "And why are you a Christian?" Perhaps each of us needs to answer that question someday, preferably in front of a European rabbi!

I opened a well-worn leather Bible and turned to that blank page between the Old Testament and the New Testament. There I had listed every Old Testament verse "proving" that Jesus was the Messiah. (I had found these in an old copy of *Halley's Bible Handbook*.) He was intrigued. "We have two hours till Zurich. Let's look those up and see what we can make of them." He opened his Hebrew Bible, and we were underway for what felt like an eternity. And there I was on a Swiss train, with an Orthodox rabbi, trying to explain the most ancient question that Jews and Christians have ever discussed. And to say the least, it didn't go well. I still have that Bible and I've kept the page as a token and reminder of good intentions gone wrong.

I thought that Jesus' messiahship was self-evident and that his fulfillment of a list of prophecies would make his identity plain. And I'd always wondered why more people in the first century never figured it out. Now I knew. It was complex.

Jewish teachers in the biblical period viewed history through a cycle of experiences. And when we see this fully played out and woven into Jesus' own identity and life, suddenly new ideas emerge. This historical cycle involves five parts: First, *promise*. God comes to Israel with a promise of goodness and blessing. Second, *settlement*. God's people settle into this promise and enjoy the goodness of God's grace. Third, *sin*. Israel departs from the covenant expectations that accompany this blessing. Fourth, *exile*. Israel risks the loss of these blessings, whether it is the land or privileges of the temple. Fifth, *restoration*. Israel repents and experiences renewal, and God raises up an anointed leader who will guide Israel to its restoration.

This brief outline summarizes every generation in the book of Judges and can be used to explain Israel's national history from the promises to Abraham to the return from exile under Ezra. And at any given time, we can ask where Israel lives within this cycle of promise–restoration. Suddenly Isaiah makes sense as he deplores the sin of the northern kingdom of Israel. Jeremiah makes sense as he provides hope of restoration after the Babylonian exile. God's promises are linked to his covenant relationship with Israel: Israel can ruin the blessing of these promises through sin, but God is faithful and eager to restore Israel to what has been promised in the beginning.

Therefore, when national catastrophe fell on Israel either through a local battle or a catastrophic conquest, Israel had a framework for interpreting their history and God's role. Had Israel been unfaithful? Are covenant blessings in jeopardy? When Hezekiah sees the enormous threat of the Assyrian Empire bearing down on the Middle East in the eighth century BC, he knows that repentance and renewal of the covenant are essential to sustain them in the imminent crisis.

During the three hundred years before Jesus, difficult and troubling conversations burdened Israel. Many had returned from the Babylonian exile in the fifth century BC, but were troubled by what emerged. The city of Jerusalem was rebuilt and its walls were reestablished, and the nation was working to reconsolidate its identity in faithfulness. The biblical books Ezra, Nehemiah, Haggai, Zechariah, and Malachi provide helpful background to this era. But the exile return did not meet everyone's expectations. The Persian Empire controlled Israel. And when the Persians fell to the Greeks in the late fourth century BC, Israel was dominated once more. Greek control waned in the third century BC, and soon Israel found itself with a short-lived, tenuous independence. But this too was unsatisfying because factions within Israel fought internally for control. Some Jews, for example at the Dead Sea community, were convinced that the leaders in Jerusalem were illegitimate and so moved to the desert to await God's judgment.

Then amid the chaos in the first century BC, the Roman Empire conquered the entire Middle East, and again Israel lived as a vassal under a powerful enemy. Its province was named Judea (Judea for "the Jews" [Gk. *Ioudaioi*] who lived there), and military rulers controlled Jewish destiny. There were occasional Jewish rulers (King Herod, Herod Antipas), but these were either puppet rulers for Rome or utterly compromised by Roman influence.

Two themes emerged from the hundred years before Jesus. First, the dream of a renewed Israel was prominent, and second, a profound desire for purity and spiritual renewal aimed to bring back God's blessing. Reading nonbiblical Jewish writings such as the Psalms of Solomon or 1 Enoch makes plain the passion for finding a person who was anointed (*messiah*) by God. Here we read a prayer from the Psalms of Solomon, likely written by a Pharisee:

> Behold, O Lord, and raise up for them their king, the Son of David, at the appointed time which you, O God, did choose, that he may reign over Israel your servant. And equip him with strength, that he may shatter unrighteous rulers, and may cleanse Jerusalem from the gentiles that trample her down in destruction. . . .
>
> He will be one taught by God—a righteous king over them. And there will be no unrighteousness in their midst in his days, because they are all a holy people, and their king is the Lord's anointed [*Christos* or Messiah].
>
> May God cleanse Israel against the day when he shows mercy in blessedness, against the day he chooses to lead his anointed one [*Christos*]. Happy are they who are born in those days—to see the Lord's goodness which he shall bring upon a generation to come. (Psalms of Solomon 17:21-24, 32-34; 18:5-7)

Notice what the prayer says. It implores God to raise up an anointed reigning figure, modeled after King David, who will use his strength to purify Jerusalem of unrighteous rulers—and here we assume these may be Jewish rulers. The prayer asks that this anointed ruler would cleanse Jerusalem of Gentiles—and here we assume a reference to Romans. The aim is to return righteousness to Judea by purging the land of foreigners who oppress it. And this will lead to a return to God's promised blessing.

What is the assumption built into these words? In the five-step cycle, Judea is still in exile—an internal exile this time, but an exile nevertheless. And only the pursuit of holiness and the help of an anointed leader will bring resolution.

This was a common expectation in Jesus' day. A desperate hope for liberation contributed to a religious passion to see Judaism redeemed and restored. Jewish writers reached back to the profiles of heroic figures of the Old Testament and there found inspiration. Many great "anointed" leaders had saved Israel; now they hoped for a spectacular Anointed Leader (a messiah) who would be a catalyst for renewal. Images were found in Adam, Moses, Joshua, David, even Elijah. In fact, the hoped-for leader virtually became a composite character, a superhero of sorts who would bring the perfection of Adam (before he fell), the courage of Moses (as he defeated Pharaoh), the skill of David (who ruled over Israel's imagined golden era), and the prophetic boldness of Elijah (who never compromised God's covenant).

JESUS

This passion for political and spiritual redemption was widespread. And it presented an irresistible temptation to those who wanted to play the role. A Jewish historian living in the first century (Josephus) describes numerous men who claimed they were anointed and fit for this task: Judas, son of Hezekiah; Simon of Peraea; Athronges the Shepherd; and Judas the Galilean are just a few of these. In each case the Romans dealt with them swiftly and violently. Even Roman historians (such as Tacitus) knew about this Jewish tendency to find and follow a "messiah" and wrote about it. In some cases, these imposters were crass self-promoters looking for power; in other cases, they used all of Judaism's religious imagery to justify their position as fulfiller of hope.

When Jesus entered this stage of Judaism's history, the country was rife with political tension. Deep skepticism about resistance held for some; others were ready to find their messianic leader and fight. Jesus' baptism evoked numerous themes in this: he begins his ministry with an act of purification (immersion in the Jordan River), the Spirit anoints him with power, and God's voice echoes the words of Psalm 2—the very liturgy used for Israel's kings—saying that indeed Jesus is God's chosen son. Jesus emerges from the Jordan just as Joshua had (Jesus' name in Hebrew is Joshua) and he enters the wilderness to defeat Satan. And in Matthew when Jesus begins his ministry he speaks from a mountain (as Moses had). Even the prophet John the Baptist, dressed like the prophet Elijah, is his promoter, announcing that this is indeed someone unparalleled coming into the world (Malachi 4:5; John 1:29). It is no surprise that the theological specialists from Jerusalem come to the Jordan River to investigate (John 1:19-28) and continue to interrogate Jesus later. If this is a fraudulent claim, then it must be judged as such.

The unfolding of Jesus' ministry in each of the Gospels reinforces this same idea. Jesus is the fulfiller of Israel's hope. He is empowered by the Spirit of God to do fabulous miracles and to teach profoundly. This is why Mark begins his Gospel with the words "good news." This term (Gk. *euangelion*, or "gospel") was a well-known designation for an official announcement. Its use by the Romans was widespread, and here Mark is happy to exploit it. The good news is that the Messiah has come, the hope that had been nurtured for two centuries is now among us, and the redemption of the people is at hand.

Just in case we missed it, when Mark (and the other writers) describe the growing awareness of Jesus' followers, the apex of this revelation comes almost dead-center in the Gospels. At this dramatic high point, we find this crescendo: Jesus asks Peter and the others about his popular identity. After a few false starts, finally Peter remarks aloud, "You are the Messiah" (Mark 8:27-30). At last, the answer is public. This is the question that the high priest wants answered at Jesus' trial: "Are you the Messiah?" (Mark 14:61). Again, the answer is made public. "'I am,' said Jesus" (Mark 14:62).

JESUS AND GOD

So far so good. Jesus is announced as the Messiah, the Christ, the great redeemer of Israel. But it remains to be seen what sort of redemption Jesus will offer. Is this redemption from the Romans? Is this hope for the poor? Is this a restoration of Israel's fortunes? Or is it something else? But first we need to take another step.

The Gospel writers were not content to leave their message with the good news that the Messiah had arrived. This was an elementary teaching by the time the church had matured and grown. There was something more here, and this too needed clarity. In a word, *Jesus was more.* This is the startling idea no one was expecting. In early Judaism, the Messiah was an earthly figure modeled on someone like Moses. There might have been a divine mission—a calling from God—but there was never a "divine identity." This would have been outrageous. Jews might call it heresy. Blasphemy. But the Gospels hint at things they can barely describe.

Jesus seems to have powers that belong solely to God. Miraculous healing was common in his day. So when a man approaches one Sabbath with a crippled hand (Mark 3:1-6) Jesus suspends the healing to ask something probing. *Should he do this—should he work—on the Sabbath?* Jesus completes the healing, and his opponents are angered. The sanctity of the Sabbath was extremely well known, and respecting it was commanded by God (Exodus 20:8-11). Is Jesus presuming on God's authority? On another Sabbath Jesus heals a man near one of Jerusalem's great pools (John 5:1-15). Again, a controversy erupts. But now the Gospel explains, "So, because Jesus was doing these things on the Sabbath, the Jewish leaders began to persecute him. In his defense Jesus said to them, 'My Father is always at his work to this very day, and I too am working.' For this reason, they tried all the more to kill him; not only was he breaking the Sabbath, but he was even calling God his own Father, making himself equal with God" (John 5:16-18). Jesus was acting on behalf of God. Or perhaps, Jesus was not merely representing God, Jesus was *presenting* God to the world.

On another occasion, Matthew tells us that Jesus once explained the inability of his generation to understand the deeper things God has to say. Jesus prays, "All things have been committed to me by my Father. No one knows the Son except the Father, and no one knows the Father except the Son and those to whom the Son chooses to reveal him" (Matthew 11:27). Here he's making an astonishing claim. As God's Son, he has access to the Father in ways no one else does. It is outrageous, or it is inspiring. But it was a feature of Jesus' self-understanding that needed to be reported.

The Gospels are making a claim that had not been heard before in Judaism. In the life of Jesus, something of God is at work. He exceeds by far the role of the learned rabbi. He also exceeds the role of the inspired prophet. Jesus is more, Jesus is unique. Quickly his followers learn that their attitude toward Jesus (discipleship or rejection) determines their relationship to the God of Israel (Matthew 10:33). Jesus will be elevated to a role of judging the world (John 5:22), and his followers will join him in this role (Matthew 19:28). This is God's role and belongs to no one else. The Gospels are exploring how God has arrived in the world, not alongside Jesus (participating in his work), but within Jesus (appearing in his life).

Therefore, alongside the words "You are the Messiah," Peter must say more: "You are the Son of the living God" (Matthew 16:16). This is not something ambiguous that may be subjected to a lesser meaning. This does not mean that Jesus is a "son" as any person is a "son (or child) of God." This is elevated language; this is an idea that Peter's Jewish language has no category for. Jesus has a divine identity—a divine origin, a divine life, and a divine destiny—and each of these is an important aspect of our confession as Christians.

By the time the Gospel writers wrote, the notion that Jesus claimed to be the Messiah was commonplace. The pressing need was to help Jesus' followers understand that more was happening here. Messiahship had been wed to divinity, the Father had visited us in his Son, Jesus was *God in descent,* and when we embrace him, we are embracing what God himself has done in the world. This God in descent was not a ghost or imitation of a person; *he was God arriving in real humanity.* The apostle John wrote a letter underscoring this every idea. This Jesus, this person in whom God was fully present, was seen, heard, and touched by the earliest Christians (1 John 1:1-4). And to deny this full union of the Father and Son is to lose something essential about our faith (1 John 2:22; 4:1-6).

The temptation of every generation has been to demote Jesus and make him a hero of our era. In past times we have met him as a sage, a movement leader, a justice advocate, or a proponent of a new order of love and forgiveness. Each of these has a measure of truth. But they miss the more important target. The Gospels have an understanding of Jesus (called a Christology) that is deeply theological. Jesus does not provide merely a fine human example; he comes as a divine visitor who has embraced our humanity in order to show us a new way. We see this temptation and its correction played out powerfully in the first letter of John.

two

KINGDOM

*The time is fulfilled, and the kingdom of God is
at hand; repent and believe in the gospel.*

MARK 1:15

Many of us want to recruit Jesus into our agenda for the
world. When asked, "What was Jesus' essential message?"
or perhaps, "What was Jesus' project for the world?" it is
common to hear things such as love or forgiveness or sacrifice.
Some see him as an advocate for justice or a protector of the
poor. These are important ideas in the Gospels, but they are not
central. When evangelicals are asked this question, they move
immediately to Jesus' saving work on the cross. In this case, it
seems that Jesus' chief purpose in living was to die as a sacrifice
for sin. And while we do not want to diminish this truth, still, a
careful reading of the Gospels demonstrates that this work, this
cross work, was not central to Jesus' teaching. For some of us
this will come as a surprise. Jesus seems to think less about sin
management than he does about kingdom building. We need to
probe the meaning of this.

If we simply study the linguistic data alone, the main interest
of Jesus' ministry comes into sharp focus. No theme occurs more

frequently than the "kingdom of God." The term *kingdom* appears 126 times in the Gospels (Matthew 55 times; Mark 20 times; Luke 46 times; John 5 times). Jesus refers to the kingdom of God or kingdom of heaven 84 times. If we allow for duplicate sayings among the Gospels, we can find about 75 separate sayings from Jesus about this kingdom. Even when later apocryphal gospels tried to represent Jesus, they knew this theme was central. The much later apocryphal Gospel of Thomas has 114 verses, and 22 discuss the kingdom of God. Matthew, Mark, and Luke each have some version of Jesus' opening salvo in his public ministry, "The kingdom of God is at hand; repent and believe the gospel."

The sheer heft of this Gospel material is enough to make us pause. No motif in the teaching of Jesus compares. Jesus' kingdom is a genuine reality with qualities that affect us. This kingdom can be entered (Mark 9:47). A person may be in the kingdom (Matthew 13:43), or near it (Mark 12:34), or far from it (Matthew 23:13). When we encounter this kingdom, it can be desired and possessed (Luke 12:31; Mark 10:14). Therefore, it is one of the hallmarks of disciples that they belong to this kingdom (Matthew 13:52). Jesus even tells a series of parables describing the mysterious growth of the kingdom (like the growth of a mustard seed, Mark 4:31-32) or its surprising discovery, which makes a person want to sell everything in order to possess it (like finding a precious pearl, Matthew 13:45).

Jesus is therefore the bringer of some new reality, some new entity that is breaking into human history. He opens his public ministry in Mark and Matthew with an announcement that the kingdom of God is arriving. In Luke 4:43, Jesus explains that announcing the kingdom is the reason he was sent—it is the imperative force of his entire ministry.

And yet there seems to be a mystery here. In fact, Jesus says as much. In Mark 4:11 he refers to the "secret" of the kingdom of

God, which he's willing to give to select disciples—but for many, its deepest meaning is undisclosed. They are left wondering about its meaning in the forest of parables and metaphors about fishing nets, fields of grain, rare pearls, small mustard seeds, bread yeast, vineyards, and fig trees. For centuries theologians have echoed the confusion of the disciples in Mark 4:10. The exact meaning of this central theme in Jesus' life seems unclear. That has to sound amazing. Jesus is central to everything. And this theme is central to Jesus. How can this be unclear?

THE ANXIETY OF THE AUTHORITIES

Certainly for some in Jesus' day this kingdom language was worrisome. The idea of a religious leader announcing a new kingdom would have set off alarms. The Roman Empire used the word *kingdom* with care. As its empire expanded Rome conquered a number of regional "kingdoms." And Judea was one of those. The old legacy of the kingdom of David still echoed in the country. Rome's defeat of the Jews in 63 BC should have put an end to this speculation (by Rome's reckoning), but it didn't. In Judea (this is the name of the Roman Jewish province) King Herod (37–4 BC) had been given his title of king by Rome. He was a king ruling his own small tribal state called the kingdom of Judea, and Rome was no doubt comfortable with this. Herod was a proxy king for Rome who loved the larger empire. He even sent three of his sons (Antipas, Archaelaus, and Philip) to Rome for an education with private tutors (Josephus, *Jewish Antiquities* 17.20-21). Herod was a king, but he was fully obedient to Caesar.

Herod's kingdom enjoyed an official endorsement by Rome. But because Herod's sons were so troublesome (and politically ambitious), the "kingdom of Judea" was eventually made into a Roman province. "Judea" no longer had a king and was to be ruled by minor rulers (called tetrarchs, rulers of "a part").

Eventually it would see the arrival of a Roman governor with imperial credentials.

Therefore, most Jewish aristocrats or Roman provincial leaders would have found Jesus troubling. Was Jesus launching a revival of the old kingdom? Did he have political dreams? Was his kingdom a political force that would rival what Herod built? Was it a direct challenge to Roman aspirations in the region? When the Magi come to Jerusalem looking for the infant Jesus, they say they are looking for the "King of the Jews." This is what triggers Herod's anxiety and violence. *Herod was the king of the Jews.* When Jesus enters Jerusalem in his final week (today called Palm Sunday), the crowds cheer and call out, "Blessed is the kingdom of our father David! Hosanna in the highest!" (Mark 11:10). This was certainly disturbing to any whose job was to suppress Judaism's kingdom aspirations. Then at Jesus' trial, the title returns when the Roman governor Pilate asks Jesus directly, "Are you the king of the Jews?" (Matthew 27:11; Mark 15:2; Luke 23:3; John 18:33). It is no surprise that this title appeared above Jesus on the cross (Mark 15:26; John 19:19). One wonders: Is the cross connected in some way to the perceived threats some felt about Jesus' kingdom and the empire of Rome?

If we think about the political climate of the first century and Rome's worries about insurrectionist movements, this theme in the Gospels certainly seems perplexing. If Jesus wanted a spiritual movement that had no army or government, it was odd that he would choose a term like this with such explosive connotations. Even some of his activities were open to misinterpretation. Once when he was on the east side of the Sea of Galilee, he met a man who lived among some tombs and was in desperate need of rescue. Demons possessed him. When confronted, the demons spoke, "My name is Legion, for we are many." Jesus expelled the demons into two thousand pigs, who rushed down a hill and drowned (Mark 5:1-13). *What does this mean?* Legion is the name of a Roman military unit. Two thousand is reminiscent of a battle contingent. Is Jesus (symbolically) defeating the powers of Rome? Is his kingdom a kingdom that will challenge the powers of the empire?

THE KINGDOM OF HEAVEN IN MATTHEW

Let's begin with an analysis of the kingdom language. In Matthew's Gospel, Jesus refers to his kingdom as the "kingdom of *heaven*" 32 times (Matthew 4:17; 7:21; 8:11; etc.). This is unusual and it does not occur in Mark, Luke, or John. Alongside this there are four references in Matthew to the kingdom of *God* (Matthew 12:28; 19:24; 21:31, 43). This means that in Matthew's presentation, the majority of Jesus' sayings employ this unexpected formula. Is there a difference? Is it important?

Some interpreters have tried to distinguish these two and have argued that Jesus is describing two discrete things here, one perhaps referring to developments in heaven (the kingdom of God), the other describing a more inclusive reality on the earth (the kingdom of heaven). But this view is likely wrong. There are places where Matthew uses the terms interchangeably, such as Matthew 19:23-24: "Then Jesus said to his disciples, 'Truly I tell you, it is hard for someone who is rich to enter the *kingdom of heaven.* Again I tell you, it is easier for a camel to go through the eye of a needle than for someone who is rich to enter the *kingdom of God.*'"

This suggests that the terms mean the same thing, since we have here a simple form of literary parallelism. But we can also find the same quotes from Jesus appearing in the three first Gospels and here Matthew simply uses a different term from Mark or Luke. Consider the parallels found in Mark 4:11, Matthew 13:11, and Luke 8:10.

Mark: "He told them, 'The secret of the *kingdom of God* has been given to you. But to those on the outside everything is said in parables.'"

Matthew: "He replied, 'Because the knowledge of the secrets of the *kingdom of heaven* has been given to you, but not to them.'"

Luke: "He said, 'The knowledge of the secrets of the *kingdom of God* has been given to you, but to others I speak in parables.'"

One very simple solution to this dilemma is that Matthew may be recording Jesus' sensitivity to an old Jewish habit that is careful when referring to God. God's name is sacred, and therefore even the Old Testament will either use the passive voice ("I was led to . . .") or use an alternate word for God ("the most high" [Heb. *'elyon*]). And perhaps Matthew is doing this. On the other hand, Jesus in Matthew's Gospel has no problem referring to "God" himself as well. The name "God" (Gk. *theos*) appears 55 times in Matthew. It may be that these references to heaven are Matthew's way of underscoring the idea that this kingdom announced by Jesus is not a kingdom that is rooted in any human or earthly effort. *This is a divine kingdom.* It is a kingdom that originates from above (not below), so his use of the term removes all confusion about Jesus' true intentions. Some scholars believe that Matthew is indebted to Daniel 2–7, where this distinction is carefully made.

The Hebrew Kingdom

Even though the words *kingdom of God* do not appear in the Old Testament, nevertheless we can find related themes. Twice the Old Testament refers to "Kingdom of Yahweh" using God's Hebrew name (1 Chronicles 28:5; 2 Chronicles 13:8. When we see a reference to the LORD in small caps, it stands for Yahweh). But more importantly linking the idea of God and kingdom was commonplace. God is depicted as a king sitting on his throne surrounded by servants and courtesans. Psalm 103:19-21 illustrates this:

> The LORD has established his throne in heaven,
>   and his kingdom rules over all.
> Praise the LORD, you his angels,
>   you mighty ones who do his bidding,
>   who obey his word.
> Praise the LORD, all his heavenly hosts,
>   you his servants who do his will.

Likewise in 1 Kings the prophet Micaiah describes his vision: "Therefore hear the word of the LORD: I saw the LORD sitting on his throne with all the multitudes of heaven standing around him on his right and on his left" (1 Kings 22:19). The primary image is of an enthroned king, reigning, surrounded by servants and couriers, even commanding an army. Jerusalem, his capital, is known as "the city of the Great King" (Psalm 48:1-3). In the Old Testament, God [or Yahweh] is given the name "king" almost fifty times.

If God was the true king of Israel, all human kings in Israel were his agents (1 Chronicles 22:10). From here it is a short step to see Israel as a kingdom. This deduction frequently occurs (1 Samuel 15:28; Hosea 1:4). But in truth Israel is a kingdom only inasmuch as it is a kingdom that belongs to God. It is never a "secular kingdom" (even though such terms didn't exist). It is a divine effort linked entirely to God's own rule. Therefore God (as king) has the power to prosper its fortunes or to bring it into judgment. He can lead it in war or send couriers (prophets) with specific words of comfort or exhortation.

Thus we discover our first major idea. "Kingdom" is not simply a common description of the political organization of God's people in the Old Testament; it is a *theological statement* about the nature of life under God. Kingdom expresses God's sovereign rule over his domain. And when Hebrew kings began to think of Israel as *their kingdom* then it would take a prophet to remind them that they were subservient to a greater king who ruled in heaven. There is almost nothing that parallels this sort of thinking about God and a nation's king in the world of antiquity.

EXPERIENCING GOD'S RULE

The Hebrew Bible sees this kingly rule of God in several forms. In one very basic way God's rule is seen in how he sustains and directs the universe. There is no anxiety about the possibly chaotic nature of the world. God directs the seasons and promises that rainfall and crop cycles will continue. The image here is that God is ruling on his throne, directing the course of nature in good ways.

It is important not to underestimate the significance of this idea. In antiquity, the natural world was not seen as benign. In most ancient origin theories, the world was the byproduct of violence and chaos, and unless humans pacified or placated unpredictable gods, the world could be a dangerous place. The God of the Old Testament brings a different message. His sovereignty *includes* the natural processes that can threaten or bless human life. Israel has confidence that the rains will come, the crops will grow, and the earth will yield its goodness every year. In the ancient world, this promise was an enormous idea. God's domain—his kingdom—would be a place of goodness.

But in addition, the God of the Old Testament is a king who superintends the direction of Israel's prospects in history. He does not leave Israel to its own fate among the nations. As a sovereign king, he masterfully controls Israel's history. Psalm 48:1-3 explains that God is not simply distant from Israel's story, but lives within it. God lives within Jerusalem's walls and reigns from the temple. This means that God lives with Israel in its crises and wars. And God is capable of bringing Israel out of any devastating experience that may threaten its life.

But we also learn that God will guarantee the future of Israel's story despite Israel's present circumstances. That is, God's rule is also an investment in the perpetuity of his people's fate. It is not simply that Israel will survive the *present* but that Israel will remain as a living people into the *future*. In Daniel 2, the prophet interprets King Nebuchadnezzar's dream by telling him that the fate of nations now and into the future is entirely in God's hands. In Daniel 2:20-22, Daniel says,

> Praise be to the name of God for ever and ever;
>   wisdom and power are his.
> He changes times and seasons;
>   he deposes kings and raises up others.
> He gives wisdom to the wise
>   and knowledge to the discerning.
> He reveals deep and hidden things;
>   he knows what lies in darkness,
>   and light dwells with him.

But there is more even still. The Hebrew prophets looked forward to a time when God would bring a climactic end to all of creation's story. Isaiah, Jeremiah, Ezekiel, Joel, Amos, Obadiah, and Zephaniah each expect a time when God's kingdom would arrive with all its fury and blessing to shift the world as we know it. Sometimes called "the Day of the Lord," this will be the arrival of God's kingly rule in full that would make all earthly kings obsolete.

This a complete vision of the complete sovereignty of God. It is instructive how much this utterly changed Israel's confidence about its own story. It would not be buffeted by unpredictable forces of nature or politics. If it found itself in jeopardy, it could appeal to God himself because he was the source of that jeopardy or capable of intervening on Israel's behalf. And in many cases Israel could pray that God would close this chapter of human history and impose his kingdom on the kingdoms of this world.

In sum, the Hebrew experience of God's kingly rule had two dimensions. God ruled the present—sustaining nature and guaranteeing Israel's present experiences in history. And God ruled the future—promising that his vision could see what was to come and his power could bring about his will. God ruled the future, and this meant he would decide how the future would unfold and how human history would end.

JESUS' KINGDOM

Jesus reflects each of these values so native to his world. God indeed sustains nature ("See how the flowers of the field grow" [Matthew 6:28]), and God's sovereign rule will exert itself in the future in a climactic way ("When the Son of Man comes . . . he will sit on his glorious throne" [Matthew 25:31]). But as we survey his kingdom sayings, we first note what's missing. Jesus does not describe his kingdom work as linked directly to the prospering of political Israel. He does not do what so many wanted—to see the kingly rule of God reasserted in Jerusalem, to see the establishment of "David's kingdom" in all its political glory. There is no interest in a political theology that promotes the idea of a new king in Jerusalem. There is no talk about reviving the royal line of David and praying for God's blessing. There were plenty of voices in this period that had this very idea. The extrabiblical Psalms of Solomon (a writing circulating widely at that time but not in the Scriptures) makes this sort of thinking explicit. This writing, likely penned by Pharisees, sought the inauguration of a new political reality that would expel Gentiles from the Holy Land and establish Jerusalem as a ruling center. And all of this would be done through the Messiah. It is striking that Jesus shows no interest in any of this. God's kingdom and the kingdom of Israel were not to be confused. This alone set back some of Jesus' listeners.

Yet while Jesus separates himself from a narrow political understanding of God's kingdom rule, still, he says that something important, something substantial, has transpired in the world. A genuine shift in time has occurred. The kingly rule of God does not simply buttress Israel's political dreams, nor is it something awaited on the distant horizon. The dramatic kingdom of God is now on earth in the course of his ministry. *Something has arrived.* Which is why the Gospel writers introduce Jesus with his inaugural announcement, "The time is fulfilled, and the kingdom of God is at hand" (Mark 1:15 ESV).

Let's illustrate this idea. In the Judaism of Jesus' day, Israel anticipated the coming of another era—a climactic era when God's rule over Israel would be expanded with the arrival of God's reign over the world. These two eras were separate, yet in the future they would merge, as in figure 2.1.

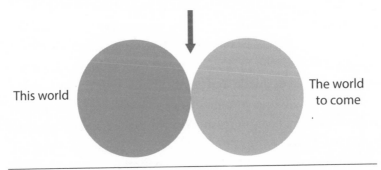

This world   The world to come

Figure 2.1

This illustrates the interruption of the present order of history, the emergence of God's powerful rule in the world, and the reestablishment of Israel as the center of God's activity. In the technical language of scholars, Judaism had a devout commitment to a "future eschatology." Here *eschatology* (Gk. *eschaton* means final, end, or ultimate) refers to the climactic events inaugurated by God's own intervention and judgment.

Now the key is this. Jesus understood this future expectation. He embraced it fully and talked frequently about the end of history and the coming of the Son of Man to inaugurate judgment. *However, Jesus shifts the Jewish understanding of what is happening in the present.* Let's illustrate.

This world   The world
                                    to come

Figure 2.2

In figure 2.2, something unprecedented has been declared. The realities of the future have now arrived *in the present.* The shadow of the future has now cast itself on the present. God's coming reign is still awaited (a future eschatology)—his intervention will be dramatic and astonishing—but his rule is now present in the world in a new and powerful way. Something remarkable has been unleashed in the world, and there is no going back.

This means that in Jesus' view, there is an *intermediate space* that exists between common time prior to the Messiah and the closing of human history on the day of judgment. This is where Jesus uses some of his most poignant agricultural metaphors. In Matthew 13 Jesus shows this perspective on time:

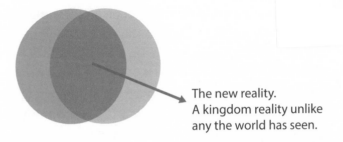

The new reality.
A kingdom reality unlike
any the world has seen.

Figure 2.3

The kingdom of heaven is like a man who sowed good seed in his field. But while everyone was sleeping, his enemy came and sowed weeds among the wheat, and went away. When the wheat sprouted and formed heads, then the weeds also appeared.

The owner's servants came to him and said, "Sir, didn't you sow good seed in your field? Where then did the weeds come from?"

"An enemy did this," he replied.

The servants asked him, "Do you want us to go and pull them up?"

"No," he answered, "because while you are pulling the weeds, you may uproot the wheat with them. Let both grow together until the harvest. At that time I will tell the harvesters: First collect the weeds and tie them in bundles to be burned; then gather the wheat and bring it into my barn." (Matthew 13:24-30)

Here the parable describes a landscape where a field has been changed by the sowing of good wheat. And we also know that one day the harvest will come to bring yield from the field. Now notice: *there is an intermediate time* when the good wheat and the weeds grow together, when the features of the old world live alongside the new kingdom. The resolution of this world and its imperfections (the weeds) is resolved only on the day of judgment.

Experiencing Jesus' Kingdom

Jesus indicated throughout his ministry that when people encountered his powerful works, they were encountering the power of this new kingdom. Once his opponents charge that he is casting out demons by the power of Satan (Matthew 12:24). Jesus takes offense at this and repudiates the charge. But then he says, "But if it is by the Spirit of God that I drive out demons, then the kingdom of God has come upon you" (Matthew 12:28). He adds that it is like the plundering of a person's house. The occupant must be bound and defeated. So Jesus' kingdom is reversing the hold that Satan has had on this world and ushering in a new order of things in ways never seen before. On another occasion he sends out seventy disciples and endows them with this same power. "I saw Satan fall like lightning from heaven," Jesus says (Luke 10:17-20). In Jesus' ministry a shift in the powers of this world is underway.

Pharisees who discerned that something remarkable was happening were quick to inquire whether this was the beginning of God's decisive intervention in history. They were thinking with a Jewish eschatology. But Jesus corrects them.

> Once, on being asked by the Pharisees when the kingdom of God would come, Jesus replied, "The coming of the kingdom of God is not something that can be observed, nor will people say, 'Here it is,' or 'There it is,' because the kingdom of God is in your midst." (Luke 17:20-22)

Note what Jesus says: the long-awaited kingdom has now arrived. It is in our midst. It is present in Jesus' life and ministry. This kingdom activity is instigated by Jesus himself. The kingdom

that is being born is tied entirely to Jesus. And thu
sition toward Jesus will determine our relation to th.. ....
So here we must underscore that Jesus was not simply a teacher-
prophet who helped men and women decipher the nature of life
or who gave them directions to God. He did both, but Jesus was
the deliverer of the kingdom of God and therefore was looking
not simply for followers but enlistees—disciples who would join
and advance his kingdom in the world. Jesus anticipated that
this kingdom was going to grow and do so dramatically but
quietly. In his so-called parables of growth, he describes it as a
mustard seed—something so small—which grows into something substantial. Or it is like yeast that moves through dough
almost magically while its full work in the bread is undeniable
(Matthew 13:33; Luke 13:20-21).

Jesus also used a series of kingdom parables that describe a
choice. When someone encounters this kingdom, all other commitments, all other investments, are put in question. It is like a
person finding a startlingly valuable pearl. Or when a farmer
who leases land discovers a treasure box buried in his field.
Everything gets sold in order to purchase such precious things.

Therefore, we can describe people as being "in the kingdom"
(Matthew 11:11; Mark 14:25; Luke 7:28). And if this is true, then
there are others who are "outside" the kingdom. There are those
who have experienced the kingdom and embrace it; and there
are those who simply have not. But once a person is connected
to the kingdom, once the kingdom reality is experienced, it is
vital to remain diligent about our commitments and the power
of God. In the parable of the sower (Matthew 13:1-9) Jesus talks
about how the kingdom of God is like sowing seed in fields.
Some seeds germinate and grow to a fruitful harvest; others fail
to realize their potential entirely.

Finding Jesus' Kingdom

In Luke 17:20 the Pharisees ask Jesus, "When is the kingdom coming?" And for centuries theologians have made pronouncements. If Jesus inaugurated something important, where do we find it?

Throughout the eighteenth and nineteenth centuries, some proposed that the kingdom of God could be found in the evolution of (Western) society with its moral values. Some talked about a "Christian civilization" that seemed to have embodied the deeper truths of the religious, moral life. This reflected the optimism of the European empires, their colonial expansion, wealth, and the "high culture" they promoted. To visit Paris, London, or Berlin in 1890 would have dazzled us as well. Some concluded that this was the flowering of human life as God intended it. This was the kingdom of God.

At the turn of the century (1900), many others disagreed. They believed that the heart of Jesus' message was a kingdom that would end the world, where God would intervene powerfully and inaugurate judgment. They believed that Jesus promoted an *imminent* future eschatology: God was almost here to end all things. Some of these scholars believed Jesus was mistaken (the End did not come) but still they insisted that Jesus perceived that the kingdom could not be domesticated into the commonplace cultures of our day. It was a foreign reality that we had not yet seen.

Then Europe collapsed into a war that was stunning by any measure (1914–1918). At least eighteen million died as well-dressed soldiers killed each other in incomprehensible numbers. And in this, European hopefulness was crushed. Religion was exploited vigorously by both sides in an effort to say that this war was God's war—and that God's purposes were in Germany (or

France or England). But the crisis wasn't over. From 1918 to 1919 the Spanish flu (sourced through the war) brought about the deaths of over fifty million people worldwide. Imagine. War and disease killed about seventy million people in five years.

For theologians, this crisis denied the optimism that so many cherished in the nineteenth century and inspired a reexamination of the kingdom of God. And responses took two directions: prophecy movements declared that the end of history had come and the future kingdom was about to arrive. In despair, they had given up hope for the world and invested entirely in a future, divine solution. Many Christians hid in their futurist predictions hoping that Jesus would simply return and end it all.

Others sought relief in a private, inward experience of God. They retreated into a personal spiritual world of contemplation and believed that the essential meaning of the kingdom was personal experience and transformation, and a readiness to enter heaven. For them, it was a present reality *and yet* it had the characteristics of the future attached to it. It was a present reality *and yet* it could not be identified with the political or cultural systems of this world.

But both of these options have weathered intense criticism in the last fifty years. Today most scholars refer to an *inaugurated* eschatology. That is, the church and its members—the disciples of Jesus' kingdom—hold a place in time that is attached to the present but also attached to a reality that comes only from God. And this new reality—and here is the key—has social and political ramifications. Something was inaugurated *in the world,* and only Christ's followers understand it and promote it. And yet, this reality has not been "consummated" or brought to completeness. There is something "already" but "not yet" in the kingdom. Imagine perhaps an early springtime in March when we find flowers blooming and snow falling at the same time.

Spring has been inaugurated, but the grip of winter is still with us. Both realities are true, yet our zeal and passion lies with the coming of spring.

This means that the systems of this world, the politics of this world, with all of their brokenness and darkness, will continue unabated. And yet Jesus announced the flowering of a new era. And therefore we—like wheat among weeds—live as Jesus' followers and become cosaboteurs with him, subverting those systems in the world that repudiate God's intentions. We become promoters of an alternate kingdom that vies with the empires of our age.

This is the mission of the church. This is the task of God's people who have followed Jesus since his resurrection and ascension. We don't simply equip people to go to heaven; we invest in kingdom building here on the earth. "May your will be done *on earth* as it is in heaven." We speak truth to power but are not seduced by the power of empires. We participate in social structures but realize their frailty—we do not put our hope there. We advance the values of the kingdom now and do not simply await some future exodus from the world when Jesus returns. We read Jesus' Sermon on the Mount (Matthew 5–7) and don't despair at the high and virtuous callings—we are inspired by them. We want a world, God wants a world, filled with peacemakers, the meek, the righteous, the pure in heart. These are not impossibilities; these are the higher callings of people who see things differently.

Jesus does not leave us alone in these efforts. The New Testament tells us that in his departure, Jesus endowed his followers with God's Spirit to empower, defend, and accompany them. We have often seen the Spirit as a gift used for personal worship or moral transformation. Both are true. But we have missed how the Spirit serves to advance the work of Jesus changing the world. In some of Jesus' final words, he explained:

But very truly I tell you, it is for your good that I am going away. Unless I go away, the Advocate [the Spirit] will not come to you; but if I go, I will send him to you. When he comes, he will prove the world to be in the wrong about sin and righteousness and judgment: about sin, because people do not believe in me; about righteousness, because I am going to the Father, where you can see me no longer; and about judgment, because the prince of this world now stands condemned. (John 16:7-11)

When Jesus' followers invest entirely in sin management and neglect kingdom building, they miss a significant part of what it means to follow him. We know what was central to Jesus' mission. If Jesus had been interviewed by the media of his day, I have no doubt that he would have maneuvered the conversation to his favorite theme: the kingdom of God. The question that bedevils the church today is whether or not we've lost Jesus' favorite theme—and how we might rediscover it, reclaim it, and promote it in the world today.

three

CROSS

*Jesus said, "The Son of Man must suffer many
things and be rejected by the elders, the chief priests
and the teachers of the law, and he must be killed
and on the third day be raised to life."*

LUKE 9:22

We are immune to the drama of the cross. Because we are
familiar with the notion that Jesus died on the cross, we
have lost the shock felt by the writers of the New Testament. We
assume that the cross was central to Jesus' mission on earth and
that his followers assumed the same. I have had students tell me
this for years. When asked, What was Jesus' principal aim on
earth? they will answer: to die on the cross for our sins. There is
little hesitation.

But none of his followers believed this for a moment during
Jesus' earthly career. When he told it to them directly, they were
incredulous. At one point Peter actually scolded him for saying
it (Mark 8:32). And in Jesus' most stern response we have recorded in the Gospels, Jesus linked Peter's rebuke to accept this
grim assignment as a work of Satan (Mark 8:33).

However, it became clear shortly after Jesus' death and resurrection that this tragedy was part of God's good purpose. John's Gospel makes this explicit: "After he was raised from the dead, his disciples recalled what he had said. Then they believed the scripture and the words that Jesus had spoken" (John 2:22; see also John 12:16). Up till that time, the cross was incomprehensible to Jesus' followers for a variety of reasons. But quickly the cross became a central governing idea that shaped the thinking of the New Testament church. All of this requires exploration. Paul even writes that Jesus died for our sins *according to the Scriptures* (1 Corinthians 15:3). What Scriptures can he mean if this was so utterly incomprehensible?

The Death of the Messiah

We learned in the first chapter that Jesus' idea of messiahship upended many of the conventions in his day. He needed to carefully reframe what it would mean to be Israel's Messiah and separate it from the various national religious causes that flourished in the first century. But there was one more element that needed reframing.

In Jesus' day, among the chief duties of the Messiah were to establish the purity of the temple and bring about an era of national renewal for Israel. The temple was the linchpin for Israel's religious life and the focal point for its national life, so the renewal of one led to the renewal of the other. Some like to think of Israel as having one city (Jerusalem) and that city having one building (the temple). In some respects, this is true: national and religious life orbited around one location. It is no surprise that about twenty years before Jesus' birth a major building campaign began to rebuild the temple and make it a monumental edifice that compared nicely with anything in the Roman world. Herod the Great (the inspiration for this effort) even hired

Roman engineers who were skilled at these sorts of things. The temple brought to Israel a life with God and this gave birth to its national life. Few could imagine a life consistent with God's covenant that neglected either temple or nation.

However—and here is what scholars know well—we have no evidence in Jewish writing during this era that anyone expected the Messiah to die *as part of his mission.* He would die of natural causes; but this was different. The Messiah was modeled after figures such as Moses, whose life (not death) brought renewal and victory. Moreover, there was no Jewish theological category of a messiah dying for anyone's sins. No notion of human substitutionary sacrifice and certainly no expectation that he would be crucified (a deeply shaming picture). There were numerous men who appeared in this era claiming to have some messianic role, and in no case was redemptive death part of their work. The book of Acts names two of them: Theudas and Judas the Galilean (Acts 5:36-37). Most died violently (thanks to Roman repression), and their deaths were crushing and confusing to their followers. In the Gospels, we can turn to a passage such as Mark 9:30-32, where we see the tension among the disciples when Jesus explains clearly that he will die when they arrive in Jerusalem:

> They left that place and passed through Galilee. Jesus did not want anyone to know where they were, because he was teaching his disciples. He said to them, "The Son of Man is going to be delivered into the hands of men. They will kill him, and after three days he will rise." But they did not understand what he meant and were afraid to ask him about it.

The idea that the Messiah would die fills them with fear and dread. They don't want to ask Jesus about it because they're afraid of what he might say. It simply makes no sense because the formula of a messiah dying *as part of his work* did not exist. We can see this despair in Luke 24 when the resurrected (though unrecognized) Jesus meets some disciples on the Emmaus road (Luke 24:13-27). They despair because their Messiah has been killed. "We had hoped that he was the one who was going to redeem Israel." There we can see the national redemptive assignment in the center of their thinking. Their despair is understandable. The redemption of Israel—the renewal of the temple and nation—would only happen when a messianic leader would step into Jewish history as had Moses or David. But in this case, their Messiah had died. This was the end of hope. But Jesus responds, "Did not the Messiah have to suffer these things and then enter his glory?" How could Jesus imagine this?

These discussions explaining the death of the Messiah were a routine problem for early Christians. The disciples on the Emmaus road needed an explanation. This likely clarifies why the so-called passion stories of Jesus' arrest, death, and resurrection were likely written first and written carefully in early church history. Jews who inquired about Jesus wanted an explanation about his death. But this question became an ongoing hurdle even in centuries to come. In a second-century essay called *Dialogue with Trypho* (penned by a theologian named Justin Martyr) we read about a Christian dialogue with a Jew named Trypho. One of Trypho's chief objections to becoming a Christian is that this so-called messiah Jesus died, and it seemed peculiar (see *Trypho* chap. 32).

However, the problem is not simply that Jesus predicted he would inevitably suffer and die, but also that he spoke of it as a purposeful death, a death woven deeply into the nature of his own mission.

A SACRIFICIAL DEATH

From the very beginning we find hints in Jesus' teaching that a tragedy would be inherent in his work. In one of his earliest stories, he spoke of a wedding and a bridegroom. The guests celebrate during the wedding until suddenly the bridegroom is kidnapped violently and everyone is thrown into mourning and confusion (Mark 2:19-20). Suddenly messianic rejoicing flips to shocking tragedy. On another occasion, he healed a man and forgave his sins and at once is charged with the capital offense of blasphemy (Mark 2:1-12). Following a Sabbath healing, the leaders of Jerusalem then plot how to destroy him (Mark 3:6). It becomes immediately clear that many of Jesus' deeds were sufficiently controversial that they led to extreme charges that could cost him his life. Jesus recognized this. Each of the Synoptic Gospels records that three times during his public ministry, Jesus declared explicitly that he was going to die in Jerusalem at the hands of the temple leadership (Mark 8:31; 9:31; 10:33-34). Most tellingly, when he came to Jerusalem, he told a parable and embedded in it this very idea.

> A man planted a vineyard. He put a wall around it, dug a pit for the winepress and built a watchtower. Then he rented the vineyard to some farmers and moved to another place. At harvest time he sent a servant to the tenants to collect from them some of the fruit of the vineyard. But they seized him, beat him and sent him away empty-handed. Then he sent another servant to them; they struck this man on the head and treated him shamefully. He sent still another, and that one they killed. He sent many others; some of them they beat, others they killed.
>
> He had one left to send, a son, whom he loved. He sent him last of all, saying, "They will respect my son."

But the tenants said to one another, "This is the heir. Come, let's kill him, and the inheritance will be ours." So they took him and killed him, and threw him out of the vineyard.

What then will the owner of the vineyard do? He will come and kill those tenants and give the vineyard to others. (Mark 12:1-9)

Here Jesus portrays himself as the vineyard owner's son who is sent after the tragic failure of previous messengers. And rather than simply being greeted with abuse, this time he is killed.

These predictions of death are less spectacular than we might think. Any prophet or advocate who is agitating the religious or political power structures of his day will run the risk of opposition, persecution, even death. It is mere prediction: when Jesus arrives at the very center of his opponents' power (Jerusalem) they will immediately want to be rid of him. And if this is all that we had from this story, it would be commonplace. But that Jesus is making a prediction that he will be killed *and* that he is the Messiah—that is unexpected.

There is more, much more. Jesus did not think of himself as a martyr. A martyr dies for his cause and his purposes are frustrated by his opponents. Jesus believed that his death was purposeful and an integral part of what God was calling him to do. *To die in Jerusalem was part of his messianic mission.* Following a dispute between the apostles James and John about privilege and greatness, Jesus explains in a critical verse, "For even the Son of Man did not come to be served, but to serve, and to give his life as a *ransom for many*" (Mark 10:45). Here we have something utterly unexpected. Jesus understood that his identity was centered on service and that his death was a feature of that service. But notice the term he uses: he will die as *a ransom*. This word (Gk. *lytron*) refers to a payment made to set a captive free.

Jesus says that his death will be a work that emancipates captives. It will be in this sense a redemptive work, a work that redeems (sets free or releases) those whom it serves.

When they arrive in Jerusalem on Jesus' final visit, his disciples sense with dread what will happen. On their approach, Thomas declares almost cynically, "Let us also go, that we may die with him" (John 11:16). The season was Passover, and Jewish ceremonies culminated with the sacrifice of a lamb and a sacred meal commemorating the great exodus of Israel from Egypt under Moses' leadership. The meal was a *sacrificial meal* since the meat consumed had come from the temple altar hours earlier. The elements of the meal had sacred sacrificial meaning for all who shared in them. It is here that Jesus took a portion of bread and broke it, took a cup of wine and poured it, and indicated that these elements were now to be sacred reminders of his imminent death (Mark 14:22-25). In the Passover ceremonies, to eat the sacrificial meat meant that they were embracing the sacrifice at the altar that day; to consume Jesus' bread and wine meant that they were joining with him in *his altar*, the cross.

Jesus was arrested during the night after this Passover meal. He was taken captive by the temple authorities, given an impromptu trial, and convicted of a capital crime—blasphemy. Then on the following day (Friday) he was crucified. The Gospel writers do not miss the importance of the setting of Jesus' death. *It took place within the context of Passover.* As lambs were being sacrificed for this meal, as the lambs of Egypt were remembered, Jesus now was a lamb whose death would bring about an unexpected form of salvation. And when this happened it made clear why John the Baptist in the beginning had given Jesus the unusual title, "the Lamb of God" (John 1:29). Jesus was a Passover lamb but, John explained, one who would "take away the sins of the world." Even when Jesus was on the cross, symbols of

Passover sacrifice abounded. His bones were not broken, blood flowed freely from his body—these were both requirements of a temple sacrifice.

Here we have two critical developments for the meaning of Jesus' death. He viewed his death as a ransom to free captives— and in the upper room he used Passover, the ultimate story of freedom, as the platform to interpret his death. He would be a sacrificial Passover lamb whose blood would cover believers from harm.

In what is perhaps the most ironic conversation recorded in the Gospels, the high priest Caiaphas worries about the impact of Jesus' popularity. Caiaphas's counselors are concerned that if Jesus has a large following, the Romans will come and destroy the temple and the nation. But Caiaphas responds with an odd sort of answer: "You do not understand that it is expedient for you that one man should die for the people, and that the whole nation should not perish" (John 11:50 RSV). Caiaphas was right in a way—he did not understand. Jesus' death would indeed be to save the people and the nation, but not from the Romans.

REDEMPTIVE SUFFERING

Jesus therefore viewed his death as an essential feature of his messianic work. It was not a human effort trying to extinguish his ministry but a divine plan for the salvation of the world. Thus in Mark 8:31 (and Luke 9:22) Jesus says, "The Son of Man *must suffer* many things." This suffering was an essential part of his service to the world. John's Gospel makes this thinking explicit. Jesus says that he is the good shepherd *who lays down his life* for his sheep (John 10:11, 15, 17). And, he says, this is a task he had received from his Father (John 10:18).

Most scholars believe that the seedbed of this idea of redemptive suffering is found in the prophet Isaiah. In the middle of the book of Isaiah we read about an odd figure for whom redemptive suffering was central (see Isaiah 40-55). We read about his anointing (Isaiah 42), his calling (Isaiah 49), and his difficulties (Isaiah 52). But then we learn that he is disfigured, despised, and rejected. He suffers profoundly and is sacrificed like a lamb (Isaiah 52:13–53:12). The context of this grim portrait is the Babylonian exile, which is about to end. In Jewish interpretation, this "suffering servant" was (and is) a corporate figure representing the nation of Israel. It is through Israel's suffering and travail that redemption would arrive. Israel would be offered up as a sacrifice on Babylonian altars, and this would be an offering for her sin (Isaiah 53:10). Through Israel's profound suffering God's will can be accomplished. Even sins will be forgiven (Isaiah 53:12) because payment for Israel's infidelities will be complete.

The key that opens our lock lies here: *in Isaiah's thinking, loss and suffering can be a vehicle for salvation.* Let's call this *redemptive suffering.* When Israel had experienced victories through power and conquest, they most frequently lost sight of their dependence on God. The covenant was abandoned. Worship was compromised. But now, in the exile—in profound sacrificial loss—something new is accomplished. God is at work bringing redemption in ways no one had expected. Healing would be found this time through pain. The suffering of the exile was thus purposeful.

This is where Jesus makes his most unexpected move. Jesus takes up the idea of redemptive suffering in Isaiah and applies it to himself. The "servant" of Isaiah is no longer Israel but Jesus. Jesus will be rejected, disfigured, and killed. He will become a sacrifice for sins, and the platform where this will be seen clearly is the Jewish feast of Passover. Jesus will become a Passover lamb and through his death, redemption will be found. Did any in Judaism think of Isaiah 53 as a prediction of the Messiah's work? No. But a close reading of Isaiah 53 will sound strangely similar to what is played out in the betrayal, rejection, and death of Jesus. In perhaps his most daring theological move, Jesus reached into Isaiah and appropriated a role from the exile for Israel and reapplied the principle of redemptive suffering to himself. The cross was to be the new Babylon; Passover would be the instrument for interpreting it. But the great gift here—and this implies substitution—is that rather than Israel suffering this loss, Jesus would take it upon himself. His life would be *substituted* for others. He would achieve what Israel needed. He would provide a messianic restoration of the nation, but it would be found through redemption from sin. Indeed, in answer to Caiaphas's observation in John 11, Jesus would save the nation from judgment.

PAUL AND REDEMPTIVE SUFFERING

The apostle Paul explains the meaning of Jesus' sacrifice more fully. In numerous verses in virtually each one of his letters, Paul touches on Jesus' death as a key to the gospel. But for Paul the cross is not simply Jesus' work. It is God's work. Since God was present in Christ and at work in Christ, Jesus' death displayed God's love for us. "But God demonstrates his own love for us in this: While we were still sinners, Christ died for us" (Romans 5:8). The cross shows how much God is for us. "If God is for us, who can be against us? He who did not spare his own Son, but gave him up for us all—how will he not also, along with him, graciously give us all things?" (Romans 8:31-32). This means that God himself, working through Jesus, present in Jesus, was achieving our salvation personally. In 2 Corinthians 5:18-19, note how delicately Paul describes the work of Christ in death as an achievement of God:

All this [the new creation that springs from the gospel] is from God, who through Christ reconciled us to himself and gave us the ministry of reconciliation: that God was reconciling the world to himself in Christ, not counting people's sins against them. And he has committed to us the message of reconciliation.

Therefore, the cross is not just a gracious gift of Jesus for the salvation of the world. The cross is a gracious gift of God, who (through Jesus) is saving the world.

Paul was a skilled Jewish theologian who knew the Jerusalem temple well. For him the context for the work of Christ derives from the sacrificial setting of the temple. So in Romans 8:3 Paul can describe Jesus as a sin offering so that judgment on sin could be successful. In Ephesians 5:2, Paul presents Jesus as a model of sacrificial love: "And walk in the way of love," Paul writes, "just as Christ loved us and gave himself up for us as a fragrant offering and sacrifice to God." This is why Paul appeals to the "blood of Christ" again and again. This is Jewish language of sacrifice in which the blood of the sacrificial victim achieves redemption. Paul writes that we are justified by "his blood" (Romans 5:9) or we have redemption through "his blood" (Ephesians 1:7). In Romans 3:24-26, which is perhaps Paul's most important reflection on the cross, Paul employs careful technical language:

[We] are justified freely by his grace through the redemption that came by Christ Jesus. God presented Christ as a sacrifice[Gk. *hilasterion*] through the shedding of his blood—to be received by faith. He did this to demonstrate his righteousness, because in his forbearance he had left the sins committed beforehand unpunished—he did it to demonstrate his righteousness at the present time, so as to be just and the one who justifies those who have faith in Jesus.

Few verses in Paul have been discussed more thoroughly than these three. The key for our purposes is to keep in mind the larger framework that Paul is using. Paul has just summarized the great corruptions that have distorted all of humanity (Romans 1:18–3:20). And now he turns to God's intervention to set things right. "But now . . . the righteousness of God has been made known" (Romans 3:21). This intervention by God is his supreme act of grace (Romans 3:24) by which Jesus has achieved and offered to us the righteousness we have lost.

When Paul says that "God presented" Jesus as a sacrifice (Romans 3:25), he is echoing the language of a sacrificial animal at a temple altar (Leviticus 1–7). And the term he uses—*hilasterion*—is critical. Jesus was a *hilasterion* on the cross. Some Bibles translate this as "expiation," which means that Jesus became an offering that deals with sin by removing its penalties. Others translate the term as "propitiation," meaning Jesus became an offering dealing with the wrath of the one offended. Certainly both are true. The word has a flexible history, and all along in Romans Paul has been discussing God's wrath because humanity's sin not only violates the law but ruptures a relationship with God.

However, this word has another important use. *Hilastarion* was employed in the Greek Old Testament (the commonly read Bible in Paul's day) for the lid on top of the box known as the ark of the covenant (Leviticus 16:2). The box was located in the Holy of Holies, where God met with Israel, that place where divine encounter, revelation, and reconciliation were made possible. In the Old Testament rituals for the Day of Atonement, Aaron the high priest originally sprinkled blood on the *hilasterion* (the ark lid) after he filled the tabernacle with incense smoke (Leviticus 16:11-14). The sprinkling of blood was the climax of the rituals of atonement.

Paul's genius was to see that the cleansing of the nation was enacted by the grand death of a person, Jesus, and that this death would have enormous consequences. Jesus' cross was that point where sacrificed blood accomplished salvation because it was an atoning sacrifice. Elsewhere Paul reminds us that Jesus had no sin (2 Corinthians 5:21) and therefore he was a perfect sacrifice. And he says that Christ then voluntarily absorbed our sin and became a curse, so that we could be found innocent (Galatians 3:13).

But how does Paul build this bridge from a ritual sacrifice to an act of personal redemption? Again the answer is found in Isaiah 40–55. The dramatic language of sacrifice in Isaiah 53 appears throughout Romans 3–5. Redemptive sacrifice, once envisioned by Isaiah, now is taken up by Paul to be the key to Jesus— and this key is recontextualized to altar sacrifice at the temple.

All of these details may seem confusing and unnecessary. But every theological expression employs the framework of some particular setting. To understand the death of Christ we must migrate to Isaiah, understand the notion of redemptive suffering, and then see its application to Jesus and altar sacrifice at the temple. Above all Jesus' death is a gift, a gesture of grace, a moment when Jesus' life has been substituted for our own.

For the New Testament, the death of Christ was a turning point in history. God had shown his righteousness by achieving in Jesus our righteousness through a dramatic act of forgiveness on the cross. In the large scheme of things, Paul and the other New Testament writers are working with a very large problem: they are resolving the problem of sin that began in Adam and corrupted the world. Through Abraham, God was at work making firm promises (a covenant) to create a people who would exemplify his righteousness and live as beacons of goodness in the world. And for Paul the fullness of this promise to Abraham, the realization of this work of God, was now found in Christ where all people— not one nation—would have access to this redemption.

THE CROSS AND CHRISTIAN IDENTITY

We need to return to Jesus. In Mark 8 after Jesus makes it clear that the cross will be his mission as he enters Jerusalem—and we know how impossible this idea was for his followers to hear—Jesus continues to say more. If Jesus' embrace of the cross seemed like an impossibility, Jesus presses the idea of redemptive suffering further:

> Then he called the crowd to him along with his disciples and said: "Whoever wants to be my disciple must deny themselves and take up their cross and follow me. For whoever wants to save their life will lose it, but whoever loses their life for me and for the gospel will save it. What good is it for someone to gain the whole world, yet forfeit their soul? Or what can anyone give in exchange for their soul? If anyone is ashamed of me and my words in this adulterous and sinful generation, the Son of Man will be ashamed of them when he comes in his Father's glory with the holy angels." (Mark 8:34-38)

In this one astonishing paragraph, Jesus says something that surely filled them with anxiety, trepidation, and shame. The cross was not only Jesus' mandate, but it belonged to his followers as well. To be clear, this did not mean that they would play a parallel redemptive role to Jesus, as if their suffering and death would achieve what Jesus achieved. But it meant that there was a principle in the cross, an idea unfathomable to the public ear, something no one had said before. Jesus' followers should carry crosses. Their life should be formed by the cross, and it only remains for us to unpack what this must have meant.

The messianic vocation centered on notions of victory, conquest, national success, and "ascent." But Jesus chose another path, a path of humility, loss, sacrifice, and descent. After Jesus' shocking revelation, he found the disciples arguing about greatness. They were seeking to leverage their own importance against each other (Mark 9:34). But Jesus corrected them: "Anyone who wants to be first must be the very last, and the servant of all" (Mark 9:35). Then he put a little child before them as a model. Self-promotion would need to be replaced by self-emptying. This is why Jesus points to children later and says that they possess the kingdom of God (Mark 10:14). This is not an act of sentimentality. This is a stark reminder that the powerlessness of children aligns most closely with the virtues of Jesus' kingdom. A rich man whose money provided great power approached Jesus and expressed concern about his salvation. Jesus' answer is consistent. The man must sell what he has and give it to the poor (Mark 10:21). The rich man must embrace emptiness and loss—poverty in his case—to approach Jesus' kingdom.

All of this set the followers of Jesus apart from their world. The Roman world despised humility. In Greek schools, children learned the great virtues of life from the Delphic Canons of Ethics, written sometime in the sixth century BC. There were 147 of these virtues, some of which we recognize today. "Know thyself" was inscribed on the temple of Apollo at Delphi. But remarkably, among these many virtues not one refers to humility. The Greeks and Romans loved what they called *philotimia*, or the love of honor. Modesty was a virtue, but humility was a shameful lowering that offered no reward. The Greco-Roman world could not imagine that humility could lead to honor.

But this is precisely what the early Christians said. They believed that Jesus' "way of the cross" was their way of discipleship. They embraced loss and suffering in the service of others as a hallmark of what it meant to be like Jesus.

Paul expresses this fully in Philippians. In Philippians 3 he outlines the acclaim and achievements he has enjoyed throughout his life (Philippians 3:1-6). But then, there's an unexpected reversal: "But whatever were gains to me I now consider loss for the sake of Christ" (Philippians 3:7). "For [his] sake I have lost all things. I consider them garbage, that I may gain Christ" (Philippians 3:8). He says these things because he wants the Philippians to raise their lives to the next level of discipleship. They are at war with one another, and their conflicts have harmed the church. And so Paul writes, "Make my joy complete by being like-minded, having the same love, being one in spirit and of one mind. Do nothing out of selfish ambition or vain conceit. Rather, in humility value others above yourselves, not looking to your own interests but each of you to the interests of the others" (Philippians 2:2-4). The "mind" Paul hopes will be formed in them is the mind of Christ, which was expressed most fully when Jesus emptied himself, descended into human form, humbled himself, and was obedient to death on the cross (Philippians 2:7-8).

Therefore Jesus' cross work was not simply a work of salvation for us, but also a mandate for how his followers ought to live. Peter echoed this as well, "All of you, clothe yourselves with humility toward one another, because, 'God opposes the proud but shows favor to the humble'" (1 Peter 5:5). It is no wonder that the early Christians had the odd habit of referring to each other as "slaves" (Gk. *douloi*, not our domesticated word *servants*) in places such as Romans 1:1 or Galatians 1:10 or Philippians 1:1. The early Christians lived in a highly stratified world where social class meant everything. But they had chosen a road of social descent that passed through the cross. By means of this they could reject self-promotion and serve those who lived at the bottom of life's possibilities. Thus Paul can write so radically and poignantly, "For we do not proclaim ourselves; we proclaim Jesus Christ as Lord and ourselves as your slaves for Jesus' sake" (2 Corinthians 4:5 NRSV).

In their best moments, Jesus' followers have fulfilled his vision for how they might live in the world. Jesus' followers have lived what some have called a "cruciform life," a life shaped and guided by the cross. When this has meant giving generously to the poor, loving the least lovely, standing with the powerless, and even sacrificing their own self-interest or lives, this reflex, this cruciform life, is what it means to reflect Jesus' kingdom in this world.

four

GRACE

It is by grace you have been saved, through faith—and this is not from yourselves, it is the gift of God—not by works, so that no one can boast.

EPHESIANS 2:8-9

O ne of the difficulties we have with the array of Christian ideas is familiarity. We hear vocabulary that has been repeated so frequently—or ideas that have been refashioned so many times—that they have lost their capacity to surprise us. This is true with the idea of grace. It has become trite. It is a name for our daughters. It appears as a motif in Christian art. We name colleges and churches with it. "I go to Grace . . ." is said as simply as "I go to the University of Michigan." Simply put, we do not see this word any longer. It is like wearing a wedding ring. In the weeks after the wedding it is all you look at, but twenty years later it has disappeared from your consciousness.

Perhaps numbers will help. In the Old Testament the idea is often translated as "favor" (Heb. *hen*) and this occurs about 45 times. We find it for the first time in Genesis 6:8: "Noah found favor in the eyes of the LORD." The idea is also found in the idea of mercy or lovingkindness (Heb. *hesed*), which occurs about

75 times. When Psalm 136 (NASB) repeats again and again that God's "lovingkindness" endures forever, we are touching on this theme.

The simple word *grace* (Gk. *charis*) appears about 55 times in the New Testament. And if we count the verbal or adjectival forms, the number crosses 200 times. And that doesn't begin to explore the weight of this word within important sections of the New Testament. We read in John 1:17 that while Moses gave Israel the law (which commonly meant "the Scriptures"), Jesus has shown us God's "grace and truth."

One of Paul's habits was to use a peculiar greeting that wove together both the Hebrew term *peace* (the standard greeting among Jews) and this Greek word *grace,* as in, "Grace and peace to you from God our Father and the Lord Jesus Christ" (1 Corinthians 1:3). Everyone knew how proper letters began. The well-educated writer normally penned "Greetings!" (Gk. *chairein*) and then offered good wishes for the person's health. Even Greek-speaking Jews did this: "Greetings and peace!" were distinctive written courtesies among Jews during the centuries surrounding the New Testament. But there is no precedent for what Paul does. He breaks with convention in virtually every one of his letters. This expression clearly became a signature greeting and blessing among the early Christians. Grace and peace. Paul says to the Galatians, "Grace and peace to you from God our Father and the Lord Jesus Christ" (Galatians 1:3).

In a word, *grace* is a key that unlocks much of what we believe. For some, it is the key, the primary key, that unlocks the great ideas we hold in our faith.

The root concept behind the word comes from the idea of generosity. Or perhaps better, it is the disposition that drives gift-giving: bounty, graciousness, liberality, or charity. The gift itself—the thing offered—is a related word (Gk. *charisma* but often *dōrea*), and we can find the two words (*dōrea*, gift; *charis*, grace or graciousness) often appearing in the same sentence (Romans 3:24; 5:15, 17). When Paul talks about what has been given to us in Jesus, he compares it with the tragedy that befell us in Adam's life. "For if the many died by the trespass of the one man, how much more did God's *grace* [*charis*] and the *gift* [*dōrea*] that came by the *grace* [*charis*] of the one man, Jesus Christ, overflow to the many!" (Romans 5:15). Generosity or graciousness expresses itself in gift-giving.

We have seen the generosity and kindness of God in that he has given us the gift of Jesus. But God's charity and kindness are the premier gifts that he has provided from the very beginning.

THE OLD TESTAMENT

One of the mistakes we make is to think that the grace of God is a feature unique to the New Testament. It's not uncommon to hear sermons or read books that decry the legalism of the Old Testament and celebrate the grace of the New Testament, or describe Judaism as bound to the law and Christianity as free in Christ. Some today think that the God of the Old Testament is a God of wrath while the God of the New Testament is a God of love. Let's begin by correcting what may be one of the most widespread errors in the church.

I recall a painful memory from my PhD program in Scotland where I was going on and on about a theme much like I've been describing: the Old Testament offers us legalism while the New Testament offers us grace. A senior professor of theology, James Torrance, took me aside and said, "Let's have tea in my office and I will explain the Bible to you." It was one of those moments you don't forget. *Explain the Bible to me?*

Torrance invited me to rethink the major events in God's history with his people. And he began with Abraham (first known as Abram). This nomadic man and his tribe had been moving between Canaan (Israel/Palestine) and Mesopotamia (Iraq) along the Fertile Crescent for many years. And the two deepest frustrations in his life had become increasingly prominent. He wished to settle down and have land that was his own. And he was childless—which meant he would have no one to carry on his name. (These are two fundamental needs in any hierarchy of needs.) This is where God met him and changed his life.

His clan has settled in a city called Haran when we meet them in Genesis 11. God knows Abraham's needs and he speaks to him generously: Abraham should travel to a new land called Canaan, where he will be blessed beyond measure (Genesis 12:2). When Abraham arrives, God speaks again (Genesis 12:7) and promises that this land will be his. After a few adventures with the Egyptians, Abraham hears God speak once more (Genesis 13:16). Abraham's descendants will be as numerous as the sands of the shore. God reinforces this promise again in Genesis 15 after Abraham reminds him (Genesis 15:2). But then we come to what is important. When Abraham hears these things, he decides to believe God *and it is credited to him as righteousness.*

Torrance noted that the last word was the key. God's promise did not wait for Abraham to achieve a degree of righteousness through his own efforts. Abraham did not qualify for the promises—he did not achieve a measure of spiritual desirability in order to be blessed. God initiated this goodness *unilaterally* when Abraham was least expecting it. No prerequisites had been met. In fact, there is more: throughout the Old Testament one marker of a person whose life is guided by the law of God was circumcision. (All male children were circumcised on their eighth day as an indication of their identity as belonging to God's people.) But in Abraham's case, he is not circumcised and would not be until Genesis 17:22-27. Therefore, Abraham is blessed by

God—deemed righteous by God—before the law of circumcision is given. Let's say that again. *Abraham found righteousness as an uncircumcised man.* Abraham experienced God's grace without exhibiting any religious effort other than believing God's promise.

What then was the basis of Abraham's righteousness? He simply believed in the promises of God and received them. In other words, the promises of land and children were not the outcome of a spiritual transaction. Abraham does not produce any merit that wins him what he wants. God simply moves unilaterally, unexpectedly, and generously.

If Abraham was the great father of biblical faith, Moses certainly stands with similar stature. In the stories of Israel's captivity and departure from Egypt (Exodus 1–20) we find the same spiritual rhythm. Israel has been living in Egypt for over four hundred years when the story of Moses opens. And yet we learn that Israel's life had been emptied of the faith and righteousness known to Abraham, his son Isaac, and his grandson Jacob. But despite their lack, despite the absence of religious righteousness, God acts *unilaterally* to save them. He equips Moses and Aaron with ten plagues that would fall on Pharaoh, he leads Israel out of Egypt through the sea, he sustains them with water, manna, and quail for three months in the desert, and then he brings them to his mountain (Mt. Sinai). This is why all Israel sings not only about their dramatic redemption (Exodus 15:1-18), but about the character of the one who redeems them:

> In your *unfailing love* (Heb. *hesed*) you will lead
> the people you have redeemed.
> In your strength you will guide them
> to your holy dwelling. (Exodus 15:13)

And here at Sinai God writes a covenant—a contract—with them. He outlines his expectations for what it means to live a life of righteousness accompanied by him (Exodus 20). But here is the key: *redemption preceded law-giving.* The law was never a requirement by which Israel might be saved; it was a response to a salvation that had already transpired.

This pattern of generous salvation followed by expectation is a rhythm throughout the Old Testament. In Deuteronomy it is repeated so that the people will remember. God's action of defeating the Egyptians and leading them through the desert *while they were unrighteous* forms the basis of Israel's response of thanksgiving and worship. When children ask about the meaning of the law, parents are to say: *We were slaves in Egypt! And God rescued us with a mighty hand! He gave us this land and he gave us hope. Then the Lord gave us these commands* (Deuteronomy 6:20-24, paraphrased). The rhythm is clear once again. Because God has acted so generously, so we act in response. Because God is faithful, so we are faithful. This is why the Psalms tell us over one hundred times that God's enduring love is what sustains us (Psalms 100:5; 118:2; 136:1). Our blessedness, our salvation, our righteousness are gifts—they are never tokens of our achievement.

These two examples from Abraham and Moses set the standard for what we know about the God of the Old Testament. He is a God of grace and mercy, of generosity and charity. If we want to read about the heartbreaking love of God for his people when they reject him, we need go no further than the prophet Hosea. If we want to hear in poetic song about the goodness of God's intentions, we can study Isaiah. The *initiating goodness* of God is commonplace throughout the Old Testament, and it forms the basis of everything that both Jesus and Paul wanted to say.

THE NEW TESTAMENT: THE GOSPELS AND ACTS

No Jew who heard the teaching of Jesus or read a letter from Paul needed to be introduced to grace. *They needed to be reminded about grace.* At the core of the gospel is that this grace—known for so long—has now appeared in Jesus Christ. And this expression of divine grace should not be missed. Therefore, we might say that the generosity of God is a presupposition of the New Testament with its roots in the Hebrew Bible. It is not a new revelation. Paul thus can say that the gospel we hold is not something novel but something promised before in the holy Scriptures (Romans 1:2). When Paul wants to reach for his best example of this ancient grace, he reaches for Abraham (Romans 4) and cites Genesis 15:6 ("Abraham believed God") as the model of everything we know about how to live under grace. For Paul, Abraham modeled how righteousness and blessing never come through legalism but "through the righteousness that comes by faith" (Romans 4:13). It would have been easy for Paul to say that if someone wants to understand grace, they should simply study the life of Abraham.

But first we need to look at the Gospels. Jesus presents these themes even though he never uses the term *grace* in his teaching. Jesus puts high value on what a person does—not simply on what they say. He once said, "Not everyone who says to me, 'Lord, Lord,' will enter the kingdom of heaven, but only the one who does the will of my Father who is in heaven" (Matthew 7:21). The quality of our faith will demonstrate itself in the manner of our living. This is a very Jewish way of thinking theologically (see James 2:14-26 as an example). So when we seek this theme in Jesus, we can see it reflected in Jesus' behavior.

It appears, for instance, in the way that Jesus treats those who lived on the margins of his world. There were Jews who had isolating diseases (leprosy) or who had made publicly judged moral choices (tax collectors and "sinners" [Matthew 11:19]). Jesus has a reputation for embracing them. In a telling exchange at the beginning of his ministry, Jesus establishes his reputation with this:

While Jesus was having dinner at Levi's house, many tax collectors and sinners were eating with him and his disciples, for there were many who followed him. When the teachers of the law who were Pharisees saw him eating with the sinners and tax collectors, they asked his disciples: "Why does he eat with tax collectors and sinners?"

On hearing this, Jesus said to them, "It is not the healthy who need a doctor, but the sick. I have not come to call the righteous, but sinners." (Mark 2:15-17)

This is our first hint of the rhythms of grace that were prominent in Jesus' life. He welcomes those who live outside the accepted canons of righteousness. He reveals remarkable grace and compassion to those whose lives are deemed broken and unsatisfactory by those who are the public custodians of what is appropriate. We have often seen these stories as examples of Jesus' inclusivity or welcome to the stranger. But they exhibit far more. Jesus has an inner reflex of graciousness and charity when he meets with those who had rarely seen it. This does not merely describe his empathy (though he was empathic); it shows a theological predisposition. Jesus believed that personal or spiritual prerequisites were unnecessary for people to encounter God and be loved by him. This undoubtedly explains the large following he enjoyed among those who felt ill-prepared to meet the criteria set out by those who promoted strict routines of religious conformity.

Jesus' parables demonstrate these same rhythms of grace. Foremost perhaps is the parable of the prodigal son (Luke 15). Here we have a fictional story of a younger son who requests his inheritance, departs for Gentile territory, loses his family fortune, and chooses to return home. Not only is he received with dramatic generosity (he never is given the opportunity to confess or "right himself") but his father even throws a party to celebrate his return. And when his older brother objects to this generosity—even when he complains forcefully—the father shows patience, kindness, and grace. In Jesus' mind, both those who have ruined their lives "in the far country" and those who have ruined their lives as they have lived within the confines of God's people are met with disarming grace. Notice carefully that parties (in this parable) are thrown not for those who deserve them but for those who do not.

In the parable of the great banquet (Luke 14) the host sends out many invitations. Trouble comes only when those who once had agreed to attend dishonorably reject his invitation. The host's generosity does not lead to his change of heart but to a richer expansion of his generosity. People from the streets, alleys, and the countryside are then invited (meaning those on the margin, likely Gentiles as well)—and those who refuse this sort of kindness are judged.

In the parable of the laborers in the vineyard (Matthew 20), the landowner hires people throughout the day: some begin their work first thing in the morning, others at mid-afternoon, and still others late in the day. The surprise comes at the end: *each worker is paid the same wage.* But of course, those who worked all day complain. The landowner answers that he should be free to do as he wishes with his money—and that no one should be offended by his generosity or goodness (Matthew 20:15). Literally in Greek he says, "Are you disposed to think of me as evil because I am good?" Or perhaps, "Do you really want to disparage my generosity?"

Luke's writings underscore this theme more strongly than any of the other Gospels. We learn that Mary's unique privilege to bear Jesus as a child occurs because she had "found favor" (Gk. *charis*) with God (Luke 1:30). Jesus is described as growing up in strength, wisdom, and the grace (Gk. *charis*) of God (Luke 2:40, 52). In Luke 6 Jesus argues that loving those who are love-worthy (who do good things for us or who live esteemed lives) brings little credit (Gk. *charis*) to us. But the prestigious life is the one that loves someone or gives to someone when they are less worthy and cannot return the favor. Here the rhythm of grace has to be visible among Jesus' disciples.

This behavior that experiences God's grace and then reflects it to those nearby is also a feature of Luke's history of the early church (the book of Acts). Their leaders are "full of God's grace and power" (Acts 6:8) and they bear a "message of his grace" (Acts 14:3). In a telling verse, Luke tells us how these leaders lived: "With great power the apostles continued to testify to the resurrection of the Lord Jesus. And God's grace was so power-fully at work in them all" (Acts 4:33). *Grace* became the principal vocabulary of Christian life in the early church with many ap-plications. For example, "When [Barnabas] arrived and saw what the grace of God had done . . ." (Acts 11:23), and "Paul chose Silas and left, commended by the believers to the grace of the Lord" (Acts 15:40). Paul's message is singular in Acts. He preaches "the good news of God's grace" (Acts 20:24). Grace is not a peripheral idea in Luke's record; it is at the core of what the church believes.

THE NEW TESTAMENT: PAUL

It's no surprise that Paul becomes the chief spokesperson for grace in the New Testament. The onset of his spiritual awak-ening was marked by God's grace. As Paul traveled from Jeru-salem to Damascus, Jesus appeared to him (Acts 9). Paul was a skilled theologian, he was working with the Jerusalem high council (the Sanhedrin), and he was a public opponent to this new movement that claimed Jesus' messiahship. When Jesus appears to him, a bright light and Jesus' voice hurl him to the ground. And when Jesus reveals himself ("I am Jesus, whom you are persecuting" [Acts 9:5]) Paul discovers that his theological commitments had been utterly mistaken. He had opposed Jesus, God's own messenger to Israel. More precisely, *he had been found opposing God himself and his efforts.* And as an opponent to God, as one who had rejected the Messiah, Paul should have been judged. But he isn't. And that is the key. Rather than experiencing the severity of God, he experiences God's grace and learns that Jesus wants him to be his chosen emissary in order to bring the grace of God to the Gentiles. Paul's life began with an experience of grace and was sustained by it for the rest of his life.

This experience with Jesus upended Paul's life and led to a rearranging of everything he would ever do. From his conversion, Paul departed for the deserts of Arabia (south of Damascus), where he spent three years (Galatians 1:18). After fifteen tumultuous days in Jerusalem with the apostles, he then departed for his home in Tarsus, where he spent about ten years (Galatians 2:1). He never returned to his old career or his old friends. He never went back to the Sanhedrin. We can imagine Paul sorting out the meaning of his life in light of his experience. The Messiah had come to Israel, was killed, and now had been raised to a new glorious life with God. An era had shifted in time. And this Jesus was the singular expression of God's grace to humanity.

After these fourteen years of reflection and reassessment, Paul entered formal ministry when Barnabas, the pastor of the church at Antioch, invited him to leave Tarsus and join him. This too was an act of grace since now others were willing to overlook his fame as a persecutor and embrace him as a pastor. But here in Antioch Paul witnessed something remarkable. Syrian Antioch was a major cosmopolitan city. Its deep-water port of Seleucia was famous throughout the Roman world, and the city had become a crossroads of culture and travel. Here a church was flourishing, and it included both Jews and Gentiles who *together* were living witnesses to the grace of Jesus.

PAUL'S FIRST CONTROVERSY

Paul's first theological surprise came when he and Barnabas (along with a small delegation) traveled from Antioch to Jerusalem in order to bring aid to Christians during a famine (Acts 11:27-30). Antioch was a major city built on a river (the Orontes), which meant that it was not threatened by the lack of rain. Jerusalem, on the other hand, had no access to a river, was dotted with cisterns to catch and retain rainwater, and looked for springs and wells to sustain itself. They even had to build an aqueduct from Bethlehem in order to sustain the city. Famine was always a threat in the mountains of Judea.

Paul had lived in Jerusalem for many years, and after his conversion in Syria he visited the city only briefly. But then many years elapsed, and for the first time he returned as a mature Christian in a leadership role. I imagine Paul being deeply apprehensive since many of his former friends and colleagues were still in the city and he had been a high-profile convert. He had served the Jewish high council (the Sanhedrin), and they would recognize him immediately. But it was the church in Jerusalem that blindsided him. Paul's delegation during this "famine visit" included someone named Titus (Galatians 2:1-10) who was a Gentile convert to Christ (Galatians refers to him as Greek). And someone in Jerusalem—we don't know whether it was the leadership— suggested that Titus needed to be circumcised. There are a variety of reasons this might give Titus pause (Galatians 2:3) but as the story unfolds, for the Antioch delegation there was something spiritually significant at stake. *If circumcision was being required as a prerequisite to receive the grace of God, Paul and Titus were against it.* This discussion in Jerusalem certainly triggered Paul because it contradicted his deep commitment to grace. Paul had received the grace of God with an empty hand—he had no religious performance to his credit when he stood on the Damascus road—and now the same grace belonged to Titus. Paul knew that this understanding of grace was deeply rooted in his Jewish tradition, and yet he wondered why such grace wasn't being offered to these Gentiles.

But things became worse. At some later date, Peter was staying in Antioch with Paul and Barnabas, and a Jerusalem delegation sent by James appeared in town (Galatians 2:11-18). These people were couriers of a similar message: Gentiles who became Christians had to submit to the law to be saved, and if they refused, the other Jewish-Christians like Peter should separate from them. Peter waffled (Galatians 2:11-12) and even Barnabas was afraid (Galatians 2:13). Paul was furious. In what is some of the strongest language we find in the New Testament, Paul confronted Peter with unsparing words. This in fact is the thrust of the entire book of Galatians. The first major theological issue to nearly divide the church was on the very idea that had launched Paul's spiritual life: grace. Here we read some of the most famous verses describing this grace: "[We] know that a person is not justified by the works of the law, but by faith in Jesus Christ. So we, too, have put our faith in Christ Jesus that we may be justified by faith in Christ and not by the works of the law, because by the works of the law no one will be justified" (Galatians 2:16).

The inspiration for the letter of Galatians came from Paul's first missionary tour (Acts 13–15). Paul and Barnabas had been successful in bringing the gospel to Jews and Gentiles in southern Asia Minor (cities such as Perga, Pisidian Antioch, and Iconium). This area we now know was the provincial region called Galatia.[1]

Gentiles in particular had responded enthusiastically to Paul's preaching. New churches were being formed, and the grace of God was celebrated. We believe that after Paul left, a delegation from Jerusalem came to Galatia, contradicted Paul's teaching, discredited his authority, and taught that the apostolic teaching required that Gentiles obey the law in order to enjoy saving grace. When Paul heard about this he penned the letter to the Galatians as his first fully polemical missive. Paul is confused ("You foolish Galatians! Who has bewitched you?" [Galatians 3:1]), and he is mad ("As for those agitators, I wish they would go the whole way and emasculate themselves!" [Galatians 5:12]). Paul knew these teachers. They had come once to Antioch. They were from Jerusalem. And in Paul's mind, they were distorting the gospel.

The good news is that this controversy found a helpful resolution. Acts 15:1-2 sets the stage. Luke writes, "Certain people came down from Judea to Antioch and were teaching the believers: 'Unless you are circumcised, according to the custom taught by Moses, you cannot be saved.' This brought Paul and Barnabas into sharp dispute and debate with them." This was now the fourth time that Paul had faced this problem. It had happened during the famine visit to Jerusalem, he faced it in Antioch with Peter, and he saw its effects in Galatia. He had had enough. Therefore Paul, Barnabas, and a delegation from Antioch headed south to Jerusalem to resolve this dispute.

The church generally welcomed them, but then we learn that a contingent of Jewish-Christians who had once belonged to the Pharisees opposed them (Acts 15:5). Paul would find this stunning: he was once a Pharisee (Philippians 3:5) and he knew that his teaching about grace fit well within the parameters of Jewish thinking. But their high regard for the law compelled them to argue that obedience to the law was a requirement for all believers whether Jew or Gentile. This debate resulted in the early church's first convocation, aimed to resolve its first theological issue. The apostles, leading elders, and no doubt many laity gathered to hear Peter speak about his early experiences (recall that he had converted the Roman officer Cornelius [see Acts 10]). Then Paul spoke about his first tour and his successes among Gentiles. But then as everyone held their breath, James (the leader of the Jerusalem church) stepped up. His speech in Acts 15:13-21 is perhaps one of the most important in all of Acts. Here James acknowledges that God's program for the redemption of the world *must* include Gentiles, and most important of all, he proclaims that in his judgment, the Gentiles should not be burdened with these matters of law (Acts 15:19). James had aligned himself with Paul. He only asked that if Jewish-Gentile fellowship was to go forward, that Gentiles abstain from things that were truly offensive to Jewish sensibilities (Acts 15:20-21).

Two delegates from Jerusalem named Judas and Silas then joined Paul and Barnabas on their return trip to Antioch. They carried a vital letter from Jerusalem's Christian leaders that signaled a generous welcome to Gentile converts and contradicted the teaching of the self-appointed missionaries of the Jewish law. With this encouragement, the multicultural church of Antioch rejoiced (Acts 15:31), and this inspired Paul and Barnabas to plan their next missions journey.

REDISCOVERING GRACE

Grace is one of the constant themes throughout the entire New Testament. We can march through almost every one of Paul's letters and find it (Romans 3:24; 1 Corinthians 15:10; 2 Corinthians 8:9; Galatians 2:20-21; Ephesians 2:5; Colossians 1:6, etc.). But it is important to remember that Paul is not introducing anything new in this. He is reinforcing an idea that many had lost. Paul's Jewish world took the law seriously and viewed it as a way to express obedience to God for his overtures of goodness. However, in places where obedience is stressed as a *hallmark* of discipleship, it is a short step from there to making obedience a *prerequisite* of discipleship. This happens in the church as frequently as it did in first-century Judaism. Fervent believers want to promote lives of righteousness and then begin to impose it on their communities. Paul is shielding the Gentiles from this pattern. He wants to challenge his Jewish audiences that recovering the grace of God is the only means to flourish personally and find your way back to the spiritual life God had begun since Abraham.

The same is true today. Societies that are driven by high performance expectations where success is measured by achievement will always struggle to understand the grace of God. For twenty-five years I served on the faculty of Wheaton College. These are exceptional professors whose talents were inspiring and humbling. And with us lived twenty-five hundred students from throughout the United States. These were exceptional students in every respect: bright, ambitious, hard working. And they were as serious about their spiritual formation as they were about their academic achievements.

But all of this came with a price: placing twenty-five hundred earnest students on a campus with two hundred earnest faculty meant that performance could suddenly become the measure of self-worth. Anxiety was as common as achievement. In 2010 Wheaton hired a new president (Dr. Philip Ryken), who said in one of his opening chapel messages something that surprised us: Wheaton needed to rediscover the grace of God. This struck us as remarkable. Most of these students came from thriving churches. God's grace is taught in required classes. Chapel is required, and our chaplain champions this grace. But something was missing.

There is a difference between the experience of grace and recognizing it as a primary Christian (or Jewish) doctrine. The New Testament—from Jesus to Paul—wants to press us to return to first principles: that God has been working on our behalf throughout history and that this has been seen with pristine clarity in the arrival of Jesus.

five

COVENANT

You are a chosen people, a royal priesthood,
a holy nation, God's special possession, that you
may declare the praises of him who called you
out of darkness into his wonderful light.

1 PETER 2:9

We are prone to think about God's efforts in the world from an individual standpoint. And to a degree this is not entirely mistaken. The Old Testament is filled with stories that describe God's personal engagement with individuals from Eve to Isaiah. This continues in the New Testament with stories that reinforce the same idea: persons matter to God (illustrated famously by Jesus' reference to the number of hairs on your head [Matthew 10:30]). We rightly say that God doesn't simply love the world; God loves you, God knows your name, God is alert to what happens in your life. This is further strengthened by the idea that individual decisions have consequences (for better or worse). Judgment and blessing fall on persons who either respond to God's call or ignore it. Therefore, persons matter.

But this is not the entire story. It is not in fact the main story. The biblical world put a higher premium on corporate (or social) life than we find in our modern (Western) world. Communities mattered. Thus, we imagine God calling Abraham in Genesis 12 and we envision him alone with Sarah moving across the deserts of the Middle East. But this isn't the case. Abraham is accompanied by an extended family—a tribal society—that he travels with and is permanently linked to. In Genesis 14 when Lot (Abraham's nephew) gets into trouble near the Dead Sea, Abraham rescues him with 318 "trained men" (Genesis 14:14). Where did these men come from? They were traveling with Abraham the entire time. We can speculate that they are part of Abraham's tribe. Much later, when Abraham seeks a wife for his son Isaac, he reaches into his tribal connections and sends a servant to "his relatives," or tribal affiliations (Genesis 24:4). The servant finds Rebekah in Nahor, and we are told that she was "the daughter of Bethuel son of Milkah, who was the wife of Abraham's brother Nahor" (Genesis 24:15). Welcome to tribal marriage.

There is a hidden key here that unlocks much of what the New Testament is saying. While persons matter, God's project to redeem the world has always found its strength in communities of people: families, tribes, nations. This began with Israel and finds its culmination in something the New Testament calls "the church."

ABRAHAM AND HOPE FOR THE WORLD

When theologians attempt to describe the "long view" of God's program for redemptive history, they begin with the story of Abraham and the tribal society that springs from his descendants. Genesis 1–11 portrays dramatically the fall and decline of humanity beginning with Adam. And it continues to record the wreckage of human life with Cain and Abel, Lamech, Noah's ark, the tower of Babel, and assorted tragic stories of life outside the Garden of Eden. In Genesis 12, the story line shifts abruptly when we meet Abram (later, Abraham), his wife, Sarai (later Sarah), and the lineage that flows from their marriage: Isaac (with his wife, Rebekah) and Jacob (with Leah, Bilhah, Zilpah, and Rachel). We learn that God's redemptive plan would be narrowly focused through the lineage that began with Abraham. It was a daring plan that worked to redeem the entirety of the world through one tribe: Abraham's tribe. This is seen clearly in the covenant promise given to Abraham, repeated multiple times (and renewed to Isaac and Jacob): Abraham's descendants will become a great nation, they will have a promised land (Canaan), and they will be a blessing to "all nations on earth" (Genesis 22:18). This nation will eventually be called Israel, and it is this nation's history that redemptive history follows. But we have to keep in mind that this tribe of Abraham was never imagined as an exclusive community whose prosperity and blessing were ends in themselves. This plan was not about Israel. But rather, Israel was a part of a larger plan that exceeded its own life and identity.

Abraham's grandson Jacob eventually had twelve sons. And when his name was changed to Israel (Genesis 32:28) the nation itself acquired this new name. These sons of Jacob eventually migrated to Egypt (the nation that ruled Canaan). When we meet their descendants after over four hundred years, they have grown to be a substantial minority in Egypt with a distinct identity ("Israelites") that threatens the Egyptian leadership. When Moses challenges Pharaoh (with ten plagues) and leads the people out of Egypt, Israel is a sizable nation, and by this time the sons of Jacob have themselves given birth to twelve independent tribes. Moses leads them into the desert away from Egypt, brings them to God at Mt. Sinai, and there establishes their national covenant. God had saved them and brought Israel to himself, and now the law was God's expectation if they were to live a life that reflected God's own holiness. What began with

Abraham's family evolved into twelve tribes with separate identities but that were nevertheless unified.

These people were a covenant people—a people with a binding contract with God. They understood the privileges of their rescue from Egypt and the obligations of their response to what God had done. The gifts of nation and land were linked to their efforts to bless all nations. Their identity was fully anchored in the promises made to Abraham. Psalm 105 offers,

> He remembers his covenant forever,
>> the promise he made, for a thousand generations,
> the covenant he made with *Abraham*,
>> the oath he swore to Isaac.
> He confirmed it to Jacob as a decree,
>> to Israel as an everlasting covenant. (Psalm 105:8-10)

The great exodus from Egypt? It was based on God's memory that he had pledged himself to Abraham and his descendants:

> For he remembered his holy promise
>> given to his servant *Abraham*.
> He brought out his people with rejoicing,
>> his chosen ones with shouts of joy. (Psalm 105:42-43)

These are the deep roots of Israel's identity. Even when they travel through the desert for forty years and enter the land of promise, Moses reminds them of who they are and where they came from. When they reap the bounty of this land and give some of it as an offering in worship, they need to recall that they are a people called to life from Abraham: "Then you shall declare before the LORD your God: 'My father was a wandering Aramean [Abraham], and he went down into Egypt with a few people and lived there and became a great nation, powerful and numerous'" (Deuteronomy 26:5).

The book of the prophet Isaiah likewise calls Israel to imitate Abraham's life and anchor its identity with the patriarch:

Listen to me, you who pursue righteousness
and who seek the LORD:
Look to the rock from which you were cut
and to the quarry from which you were hewn;
look to Abraham, your father,
and to Sarah, who gave you birth. (Isaiah 51:1-2)

Therefore, in the Old Testament three things become clear. First, Abraham is known as the father of the Israelite people (Genesis 25:19; Exodus 3:6; Deuteronomy 1:8; Joshua 24:3; Luke 19:9; Galatians 3:7; James 2:20-21; Mishnah, *Taanit* 2.4). Throughout Israel's national life both as tribes and as a nation with kings, they were reminded and challenged that they needed to live lives in concert with their fullest identity linked to Abraham (Isaiah 51:2; Jeremiah 33:26; Hebrews 11:8, 17). Second, Abraham is the source of blessing for the nation (Genesis 26:24; Numbers 32:11; Deuteronomy 1:8). The promise of the future is anchored in the covenant God had sworn to Abraham (1 Chronicles 16:16; Psalm 105:8-9; Micah 7:20). And third, Abraham's name is used to indicate the God whom Israel worships. He is "the God of Abraham" (Genesis 28:13; Exodus 3:6; 1 Kings 18:36; 2 Chronicles 30:6; Psalm 47:9; Luke 20:37; Acts 3:13).

Think of it in this manner: Abraham is the root of an ancient and strong olive tree. And Israel—the children who came from Abraham's lineage for centuries—are like branches filling this tree. The purpose of this tree was not the tree itself but how it might provide a witness to the world, how it might bless every tree or nation. The tree had a wider redemptive purpose.

As each century advanced, Abraham was increasingly venerated. Exaggerated stories were told about his wisdom and ability. One Jewish writing from the years before Jesus says that Abraham knew the law and was obeying it even before Moses had given the law to Israel! One Jewish account says, "Abraham our Father performed the whole Law before it was given, for it is written, '[this is true] because Abraham obeyed my voice and kept my charge, my commandments, my statues, and my laws'" (Mishnah, *Qiddushin* 4.14).

In a Jewish book written near the time of the New Testament (called The Book of Jubilees) we can find a retelling of Israel's story that includes fantastic literary changes. In Jubilees we get a glimpse of how a creative Jewish imagination could retell the story of Genesis and explain the life of Abraham. Jubilees says: "Abraham was perfect in all of his actions with the Lord and was pleasing through righteousness all the days of his life" (Jubilees 23:10).

But most importantly, Abraham was known as the great "father" of Israel—the ancestor from whom every subsequent living Jew would take up an identity. Another Jewish book from the same era, the Psalms of Solomon, puts it succinctly: "God, you chose the descendants of Abraham to be above all the nations" (Psalms of Solomon 9:8-9). To be attached to Abraham is to have a select place in the human family.

Some Jews living in Jesus' day wanted to portray Abraham in the best possible light for Roman readers. The Book of Jubilees says that Abraham achieved all the great virtues of Roman life. He exceeded Plato in his philosophical achievements. And perhaps if Greeks and Romans really understood the greatness of Abraham, they would esteem the Jews who descended from him. Abraham was the bringer of high culture—an astronomer, an astrologer, a philosopher, and a leading opponent to idolatry (Jubilees 11:16-17; 12:1-5, 16-17).

ABRAHAM AND THE NEW TESTAMENT

All this background is important because of the premier place the New Testament gives to Abraham. It now makes perfect sense. Abraham is a central figure. When Paul defines himself in Romans 11:1 he says, "I am an Israelite myself, a descendant of Abraham, from the tribe of Benjamin." His immediate cultural affiliation is with the tribe of Benjamin, but his deeply rooted identity is in Abraham, the "father" of the Jews (Romans 4:1). And to all Christians (including Gentiles), Paul makes the same claim: "If you belong to Christ, then you are Abraham's seed, and heirs according to the promise" (Galatians 3:29). It is no wonder that Abraham is mentioned seventy-two times in the books of the New Testament. All four Gospels mention him, as do the book of Acts and many of Paul's letters, as well as Hebrews, James, and 1 Peter. The reason for all this attention is that Abraham was talked about everywhere in first-century Judaism. The New Testament picks up on this interest in three unique ways.

First, many Jews believed that there was a link between Abraham and the Messiah. We get a glimpse of this idea when Jesus is having a debate in Jerusalem, recorded in John 8. Jesus says to his Jewish opponents,

> "Your father Abraham rejoiced at the thought of seeing my day; he saw it and was glad."
> "You are not yet fifty years old," they said to him, "and you have seen Abraham!"
> "Very truly I tell you," Jesus answered, "before Abraham was born, I am!" At this, they picked up stones to stone him, but Jesus hid himself, slipping away from the temple grounds. (John 8:56-59)

Of course, Jesus has just made an outlandish claim of priority over Abraham, and this infuriates his audience. But in addition, we have the distinct recognition that there is a link between the Messiah and Abraham. This was a common teaching in the Jewish world of Jesus. Abraham could see the future, and this included the coming Messiah himself. Which explains how Jesus and Abraham might recognize each other.

Second, the New Testament echoes a debate that asked how someone qualifies to be a "child of Abraham." Was it simply blood-lineage? Or was it more? Did you have to share the faith of Abraham in order to be truly part of his tribe? Jewish writers were already asking these questions. According to one Jewish writing, a Jew had to participate substantially in the qualities of Abraham's life to be known as his disciple (Mishnah, 'Abot 5.19). In other words, faithfulness was important. Or put another way, ethnic attachment to Abraham could be annulled if a person no longer "lived like Abraham." Someone might be ethnically Jewish, but it was another matter, as the rabbis put it, whether they were a "disciple of Abraham." Only Abraham's disciples enjoyed the blessings of this world and the next. John the Baptist echoed this when he confronted some Jewish leaders who shared little of the faith of Abraham. "And do not think you can say to yourselves, 'We have Abraham as our father.' I tell you that out of these stones God can raise up children for Abraham" (Matthew 3:9). Jesus lodges this same complaint in Jerusalem when his opponents say, "Abraham is our father!" (John 8:39). Jesus challenges their claim because their plot to kill him has disqualified their status and attachment to Abraham.

This is what Paul means in Romans 9:6-7 when he writes, "For not all who are descended from Israel are Israel. Nor because they are his descendants are they all Abraham's children." Paul illustrates this by pointing to the story of Isaac (Abraham's heir) and Ishmael (his concubine's son). The illustration is a prophetic warning indicating the limits of resting in Abraham as your ancestor. In Romans 2:25, Paul even says that someone's circumcision can become uncircumcision, which is Jewish code for the jeopardy that one enters when they forget that "true circumcision" is a matter of the heart (Romans 2:28). A claim to historic heritage had to be wed to a genuine attachment to God by faith.

Third, the New Testament makes a claim on the lineage of Abraham that is nothing less than astounding. It weaves these two other applications together into an entirely new tapestry. If faith is a necessary criterion for attachment to Abraham, *faith in Jesus* is the ultimate test of attachment to Abraham. In Galatians Paul makes the claim that Gentiles may be legitimate members of God's covenant community, but he does this with a remarkable argument. Abraham, he points out, received the promises of God for himself *and his offspring (or seed)*. "Seed" is singular here, and even though it is a collective singular, Paul tells us there is a secret hidden here in Genesis. The true seed (singular), the true heir of Abraham's legacy, is Jesus (Galatians 3:15-18).

The implicit logic is that if one wants to be attached to Abraham, one has to be attached to Jesus. *In the messianic era, faith in Christ brings identity in Abraham.* This means that Gentiles (with messianic faith) may join Jews (with messianic faith) in a new covenant family of God. In Romans 4 Paul goes further. He shows that the covenant blessing came to Abraham when he was uncircumcised. It was entirely based on faith, and the purpose of this, Paul argues, is to make Abraham "the father of all who believe but have not been circumcised," for example, Gentiles (Romans 4:11). This makes Abraham "the father of all," that is, the father of all who share faith in Jesus the Messiah. Paul says this explicitly in Galatians 3:29: "If you belong to Christ, then you are Abraham's seed, and heirs according to the promise." Since the key to understanding Abraham is the faith he exhibited, we should also see that it is people of faith who are his heirs.

We have to pause to take this in. In the debates between the earliest Christians and the nonmessianic Jewish communities, this idea that in some manner a hybrid gathering of messianic Jews and Gentiles could make a direct lineal claim on Abraham was nothing short of scandalous. The promises, privileges, and mission of Israel were in some manner being fulfilled by the fledgling gathering called the church. When Peter addresses Gentile Christians with these words—"But you are a chosen people, a royal priesthood, a holy nation, God's special possession, that you may declare the praises of him who called you out of darkness into his wonderful light" (1 Peter 2:9)—he is echoing this astonishing claim. He reassures these Gentiles by affirming their full inclusion into Abraham's family: "Once you were not a people, but now you are the people of God" (1 Peter 2:10).

THE NEW COVENANT COMMUNITY

This roundabout tour through Abraham may seem laborious. But we need to return to the first century and hear how messianic debates within a synagogue might have sounded. It is essential for understanding one of the fundamental claims of the New Testament. *The redemptive covenant community that began with Abraham now finds its messianic fulfillment and expression in the community of Christ.* If God was using the tribe of Abraham to pursue the redemption of the world, that tribe has evolved in utterly unexpected ways. Jews have not been excluded. They have been invited in. God's faithfulness to the historic tribe of Abraham can be found in the many Jews such as Paul who recognize the Messiah, believe in him, and follow him (Romans 11:1-6). But also, now (and this is the fullest miracle) Gentiles have been invited in equally if they too celebrate the Messiah by faith. In Ephesians Paul describes this dramatically. Gentiles had always been alienated from the nation of Israel

(Ephesians 2:12). But those who were "far off" (that is, Gentiles) have been brought near. In the blood of Christ, God has made both Jews and Gentiles into "one new person" (Ephesians 2:15, author's translation) thereby making peace. Those who are "near" (Jews) and those who are "far" (Gentiles) now in Christ share a new reality in a new community.

Recall that Abraham in Genesis 12:1-3 received three promises from God: that he would have numerous children, that he would have land on which to build a great nation, and that he would be a blessing to the "nations," that is, those outside Israel. For Paul, the inclusion of "the nations" into the tribe of Abraham is the fulfillment of this third promise of Genesis 12. Paul writes, explicitly echoing Genesis 12, "Scripture foresaw that God would justify the Gentiles by faith, and announced the gospel in advance to Abraham: 'All nations will be blessed through you.' So those who rely on faith are blessed along with Abraham, the man of faith" (Galatians 3:8-9).

A good opponent of Paul might demand that he justify this theological move. Is God now invested in a select number of Jews (with Gentiles) to advance his mission? Is it only messianic Jews that count? And here Paul reaches into the Old Testament with a concept that is as old as the exodus story. Paul indicates that within Abraham's lineage there have always been those who embraced God's covenant and those who did not. Some Israelites departing Egypt died in the wilderness and never entered the Promised Land. Citing Isaiah, he shows that throughout history only a remnant of God's people ever celebrated his mission. Paul quotes Isaiah: "Though the number of the Israelites be like the sand by the sea, only the remnant will be saved" (Isaiah 10:22; Romans 9:27). Citing Hosea, he shows that this has led to an invitation to non-Israelites: "In the very place where it was said to them, 'You are not my

people,' they will be called 'children of the living God'" (Hosea
1:10; Romans 9:26).

The image of an ancient olive tree representing the redemptive
legacy of Abraham's tribe actually belongs to Paul (Romans
11:17-24). Abraham is the root of this tree. Its branches are the
many who share Abraham's faith while also sharing in his lineage
(Israel). But now in the messianic age, natural branches have
been broken off (Romans 11:17, 19), and wild branches have been
grafted in (Romans 11:17) because the dramatic test of attachment to Abraham is now found in our attachment to Christ.
For Paul this should humble every Gentile and serve as a prophetic warning to the so-called natural branches.

THE CHURCH OF CHRIST AND THE
COVENANT COMMUNITY

This is where we have been leading from the beginning. The
church that we know so well is thus not simply a collection of
believers who have faith in Jesus. It is a community of men and
women who are living out the mission given to Abraham four
thousand years ago. The church is thus the "tribe of Abraham"
now joined to a messianic mission that began with Jesus. The
olive tree has branched out into unexpected places, and the
blessings it produces have reached the entire world. Wild olive
shoots have been grafted in to join the natural branches while
some of the natural branches have been broken off (Romans
11:17). But the end result has been a living tree, a redemptive tree,
that brings hope to the world. In this manner, the third promise
to Abraham is now complete.

The key to understanding what has happened lies in what
Jesus did in the upper room in the last week of his life. Abraham's
shared commitment with God was confirmed though a covenant. It was a binding promise that was sealed with a sacrifice

(Genesis 15:8-17). And at this point in God's plan, with the arrival of the Messiah, we should expect the same: another binding promise sealed with sacrifice. At this critical juncture, where a new messianic arrangement between Jews and Gentiles begins, another covenant is inaugurated. This is the deepest meaning of what transpires in the upper room when Jesus announces that his impending death will sacrificially confirm a "new covenant" between God and his creation (Luke 22:20; 1 Corinthians 11:25; 2 Corinthian 3:6; Hebrews 9:15; 12:24). "This cup is the *new covenant* in my blood." A new binding rule is now at work that echoes the covenant of Abraham and yet expands it richly. The book of Hebrews employs Jeremiah 31:31-34 to show that this had been anticipated from the beginning: "I will establish a *new covenant* with the people of Israel . . . *not like the covenant I made with their ancestors.*" And then Hebrews goes on to say, "By calling this covenant 'new' he made the first one obsolete" (Hebrews 8:13). Tectonic shifts are underway that respect the legacy of Abraham, that build on the promises he enjoyed, and yet in the messianic era, something new has happened. The blessing of the Gentiles has now begun.

Paul is not unaware of Abraham's other two promises: Abraham will have many descendants and Abraham's people will have land. But what we see happening is that these promises are deepened and broadened. The fantastic growth of the tribe of Abraham now includes children who live throughout the Mediterranean and who claim ancestries that are Galatian, Roman, and Arab. Peter makes this clear in his Pentecost speech (Acts 2:7-12) when the gift of the Spirit is expressed in speech that is heard not simply as Aramaic but as language that Parthians, Cappadocians, Egyptians, and Cretans can understand. But Jews will understand it as well. This new messianic movement—the movement driven by Abraham's children—will embrace diverse cultures. This is the root meaning of Paul's assertion in Galatians 3:26, "You are *all* children [Gk. *sons*] of God."

But what about the land promises? This too was part of Abraham's covenant. If the identity of his descendants was undergoing a shift, what about Canaan? In one of Paul's most dramatic moves, he shows his awareness of the land promise of Genesis 17:8, but then he shifts its words. "It was not through the law that Abraham and his offspring received the promise that *he would be heir of the world*, but through the righteousness that comes by faith" (Romans 4:13). The world? What happened to Canaan? The domain of Abraham's descendants now is no longer limited to the Holy Land. It encompasses the entire world because Abraham's children born by faith in Jesus now live throughout the globe.

Therefore, in Galatians 3:28 we can see Paul undermining privileges that people often claim but now in Christ should dissipate. There are no privileged distinctions in gender (male/female), social status (slave/free), or ethnicity (Jew/Greek) within the body of Christ. Of course, differences remain in these categories, but in the gospel, advantages disappear because Christ has created a new community. The female Greek slave (markers in a Jewish worldview that demoted social status) could stand alongside the male Jewish free citizen of Rome.

This one insight—that the children of God now welcome every ethnicity in every land—lies at the heart of the early church's mission to the Gentiles. It was not to be a community that was ethnically exclusive. This lesson was difficult for early Jewish Christians to understand. But Peter's vision of a sheet and "clean and unclean" animals (Acts 10) confirmed the new vision. Peter's objection is met with these timeless words: "Do not call anything impure that God has made clean" (Acts 10:15; 11:9). That Peter understands this new way of framing the world—abandoning tribal reflexes, embracing global instincts—is proven when he moves directly to the Gentile city of Caesarea and converts the Roman officer Cornelius.

Telling also is Stephen's long speech in the book of Acts (Acts 7:1-53). It is no surprise that Stephen's words are met with outrage (Acts 7:54-60) because in them he declares that the so-called pillars on which first-century Judaism stood were now under reconstruction. The Holy Land (defended tirelessly) now includes Egypt and Mesopotamia. The temple (celebrated endlessly) had a misplaced importance. And the Scriptures (obeyed diligently) will become the basis of judgment instead of a place of refuge because their readers had failed to embrace Jesus. Stephen is upending the assumed categories of nonmessianic religious identity. His audience understands it perfectly. And for it, they kill him.

The church therefore is a continuation of the tribe of Abraham—now known as the messianic Abrahamic community—that is fully and completely inclusive. The promises to Abraham have been widened and deepened. And the church now takes up this call to redeem the world. It is not a new calling; it is an ancient calling that began in Genesis 12.

This new Abrahamic identity also explains why the church appropriates language and categories that belong in the Hebrew Bible. The church is now "God's people" (Romans 8:27; 2 Corinthians 13:13; etc.). Moreover, the church is "God's temple." This is explained clearly when Paul writes to the Corinthian church, "Don't you know that you yourselves are God's temple and that God's Spirit dwells in your midst? If anyone destroys God's temple, God will destroy that person; for God's temple is sacred, and you together are that temple" (1 Corinthians 3:16-17). These words are nothing short of stunning. We have to pause and think about how they would sound among Paul's Jewish friends. An ancient legacy is experiencing redefinition. This further explains why Christians have license to use the Hebrew Bible as if it were our own. We can

cite Isaiah 12:2 in worship—and while it was originally directed
to an Israelite audience, now since we in the church belong to the
Abrahamic tree, we may employ it in worship.

> Surely God is my salvation;
> I will trust and not be afraid.
> The LORD, the LORD himself, is my strength and my defense;
> he has become my salvation.

It is important to remember that within the New Testament,
the church is never described as replacing ethnic Israel. The
church from its beginning was a movement birthed from *within*
Israel. The earliest church was Jewish. These were Jews who embraced the Messiah Jesus and invited Gentiles to join. But the
New Testament is also aware that as the church increased its
Gentile population and as Jewish rivals solidified their opposition, anti-Semitism might emerge. In Romans 10–11 Paul is
explicit in his warning about this. In his olive tree metaphor, the
grafted-in branches must not boast over the natural branches.
Paul still believed in the salvation of "all Israel" (Romans 11:26)
for the sake of their ancestry (Romans 11:28). But he is unclear
how this will happen. Certainly, he does not mean salvation
without Jesus. He likely expects that either through the preaching
of the church, all Israel will come to faith, or at some future date,
perhaps at the close of history, Israel will at last embrace Jesus.
However, in the present time, the church and ethnic Jews should
see each other as cousins sharing mutual respect because of
their common identity in Abraham.

REDISCOVERING AN ABRAHAMIC CALLING

It often feels as if the church has lost its way in the world. For
some, it is a community of refuge where people who have been
abused or abandoned by the world can find hope and healing.

For some, the church is a place that sustains and protects its own cultural or traditional identity so that its members will not be stained by the world. Still others believe the church's sole purpose is to worship and glorify God.

In certain respects, each of these bears a degree of truth. The pitfall for the church is that while it wants to celebrate its covenant with God given through Jesus, it can step into the same trap the Hebrew prophets identified for Israel. *The people who belong to Abraham are a redemptive community for the world.* This is God's agenda to set right what is wrong with his creation. This must include introducing people to the gospel. But it cannot end there. It means working to transform the world so that creation itself begins to align with God's purposes. "Thy kingdom come, thy will be done, *on earth as it is in heaven.*" The church becomes the church when it understands clearly its legacy, stretching back as far as Abraham, and when it recognizes that the privileges of its divine life are not simply self-serving. Its calling (like that of Abraham) is to "bless the nations," to bring light and life to the world.

six

SPIRIT

*If anyone does not have the Spirit of
Christ, they do not belong to Christ.*

ROMANS 8:9

I imagine that if we visited one of the earliest Christian communities in the late first century, much of it would come as
a surprise. Of course, we would expect to find differences in
language, dress, gathering spaces, and hymns. These are cultural
expressions. The Scriptures would be central. Clear leadership
in the form of deacons, elders, and (perhaps) bishops would be
well-established. New converts would be baptized and the Lord's
Supper (using one wine-filled chalice and common baked bread)
would be common. But if we remained a while we would see that
there was a fundamental orientation to their experience with
God that may or may not resonate with what we know today.
The ultimate test of discipleship would have been less about what
we know and more about what *we have experienced.* And in our
highly cognitive world, we would find it surprising.

In the early church, the vocabulary of Spirit-experience was
common. The gifts of the Spirit were the backbone of the
church's vitality and service. Prominent stories such as

Nicodemus's conversion (John 3) or the Ephesian disciples who lack the Spirit (Acts 19) were case studies on what it meant to be a follower of Jesus. An arresting quote from Paul in Romans 8—"If anyone does not have the Spirit of Christ, they do not belong to Christ"—may have been central to these Christians' self-understanding. They would know one of Jesus' final promises: he would ask the Father, who would send the Spirit to them (John 14:16), something that the world could not have (John 14:17). And they treasured the story of the Spirit's first descent on Peter and thousands of new believers (Acts 2). We would see all of this and possibly be inclined to call this community *charismatic* or *pneumatic*—a community centered on the Holy Spirit. This is what we need to explore.

We have seen that the essential message of the New Testament is that a new epoch in human history has begun. Expectations described in the Old Testament have been fulfilled. The Messiah has arrived. A new kingdom with otherworldly values is being born in the world. And a new community made up, miraculously, of Jews and Gentiles is growing in cities throughout the Mediterranean. Too often we have reduced the significance of what has happened until it means little more than a fresh experience of God's love and the forgiveness of sins through Jesus' death on the cross. We have reduced the gospel to a program of sin management. And we have lost the drama of the redemption story that is at the heart of the Bible. This drama is not simply about bringing us to heaven. It is about bringing heaven to earth, or more precisely, placing the world in alignment with God's wishes for his creation. The drama is about restoration. It is about making things right when they've gone terribly wrong. God has called together a community of saboteurs and conspirators (followers of Jesus) who will work to make it so.

I find it interesting that this *narrative of redemption* is inspiring to younger Christians in their twenties and thirties. They have their own narratives, and they want those stories woven into God's story, which is being written in the world. It is older Christians who often fail to see the importance of this wider story. For them the New Testament message is about personal salvation, transformation, and evangelization. Nobody would argue with this. The problem is not that it is wrong but that it is incomplete. Or worse, it has a limited view of what God is up to. God is not simply taking back our souls; he is taking back his world.

But it isn't as if God has delivered this assignment to Abraham, Jesus, and their followers and abandoned them. God's own participation within this drama has been part of this story from the beginning. *God intervenes or intersects this drama regularly.* And it is this intersection that we now need to examine. This is what we need to understand: why the earliest Christians were a Spirit-inspired community.

THE OLD TESTAMENT AND THE SPIRIT

The New Testament presupposes that we know something about the relationship of God to his creation. The foundation of this "something" is found in the Hebrew Bible and in the Judaism of Jesus' world. Two ideas from the first century were firmly rejected. First, the early Christians rejected the idea that God was so separate from his creation that he did not create it himself or that he would not enter it personally. This idea came from the notion of God's perfection and the imperfection of the world. God was light; the world was in darkness. God was "far above," we lived "far below." This idea (called dualism), so common among the Greeks and Romans, essentially severed God from his own world.

Second, these first Christians rejected the idea that God inhabited creation—that he was indistinguishable from creation and he simply animated the world and all of its life. This came from the notion of the totality of God's existence and the idea that nothing could exist without some divine life within it. This view might choose to think about "the spirit" as the animating force of creation. This would be a naturalistic explanation of something that is anything but natural. The problem is that God became indistinguishable from creation. The early Christians argued that God *created* the world but did not live within the things he created.

The biblical imagination worked to delicately balance the idea of God's sovereignty over creation and his separation from it. In the ancient world, it was easy to slip off into a variety of errors, and we even hear them today. Many today think of the life they live as animated by a "spirit" (lowercase *s*) that provides them with a divine link to heaven. This is precisely the worldview the Bible rejects. Others think that God does not appear in his creation at all and lives in some indecipherable place beyond our reach. This too is wrong.

Note how carefully the first chapter of the Bible describes God and his world. God creates it and observes it; he is near to it but is separable from it. Genesis 1:2 describes how the Spirit of God moved (or hovered) over the newly formed waters. In Hebrew the term for Spirit is the same as the word for wind (Heb. *ruah*). So from a Hebrew perspective, the wind—agitating creation, moving mysteriously across the face of the earth, uncontrollable, bringing storm and calm—was a reflection of God's universal yet distinctive presence. In Psalm 18:15, with a little poetic license, we read that the wind that opened the sea during the exodus was a "blast of breath from [God's] nostrils!"

But the Hebrew Scriptures took another vital step. God's presence in the world is indeed universal, but it is also focused and deliberate. The Scriptures describe how the God of creation moves intentionally and distinctively toward and into his creation. God reaches into his world strategically and powerfully in order to make himself known and to direct the paths of his people. This divine power, this unquantifiable presence, which is so different from anything in the world, is known as the Spirit of God. It is a power that comes from "above" and not from "below." It originates from heaven and not from creation. In the Old Testament, this Spirit was not universally present; it was *selectively* present among God's people as it shaped their lives. A simple (and overlooked) example is Bezalel the son of Uri. When Moses was with Israel in the wilderness of Sinai, God directed the nation on how the tabernacle, or tent, was to be built. Particular people were set apart and given divine gifts to accomplish what they must.

> Then the LORD said to Moses, "See, I have chosen Bezalel son of Uri, the son of Hur, of the tribe of Judah, and I have filled him with *the Spirit of God*, with wisdom, with understanding, with knowledge and with all kinds of skills—to make artistic designs for work in gold, silver and bronze, to cut and set stones, to work in wood, and to engage in all kinds of crafts." (Exodus 31:1-5)

The idea here is not simply that Bezalel is a good craftsman but that he also is appointed and equipped by God to accomplish some divine purpose in the world, namely, decorating and designing the details of God's tabernacle.

This idea of purposeful anointing with God's Spirit was well known and applied to a number of distinctive leaders in Israel's history. The most prominent were Israel's kings. In 1 Samuel 16:12-13 we have an illustration from the selection of David as king. After reviewing the many sons of the family of Jesse in Bethlehem, God directs the prophet Samuel to choose young David. The prophet came to David and anointed him with oil, and God's power entered him.

> So he [Samuel] sent for him and had him brought in. He was glowing with health and had a fine appearance and handsome features.
>
> Then the LORD said, "Rise and anoint him; this is the one."
>
> So Samuel took the horn of oil and anointed him in the presence of his brothers, and from that day on the Spirit of the LORD came powerfully upon David. Samuel then went to Ramah.

The reverse is also true. In this case, David's rise to kingship was accompanied by the demise of King Saul. This was hallmarked not by political maneuverings but by the departure of the Spirit of God from Saul's life (1 Samuel 16:14). But the pattern is consistent: key leaders in Israel's history are chosen and anointed by God to accomplish his purposes. Priests are anointed (Exodus 29:7; Psalm 133:2) as are prophets (1 Kings 19:16; Numbers 24:2; 2 Chronicles 24:20). These are instances when God provided a unique and particular gift of power to these persons to direct Israel's national life. The anointing was particular to the person and to the office they held—but it was also temporary as that person fulfilled their tasks. In a beautiful poetic passage, Isaiah looks back on the era of Moses and notes how God "strengthened the arm" of Moses by releasing his Spirit, thereby enabling Moses to achieve the great miracles of Egypt (Isaiah 63).

The unexpected feature of the Old Testament is its view of the future, in which the Spirit would play a prominent role inaugurating a new era in Israel's history. In order to understand this, we have to reclaim the worldview that was so well known in the late Old Testament. The shock of military conquest and exile, first in the eighth century BC and then again in the sixth century BC, brought the idea of disaster and recovery into Israel's thinking prominently. By the time Israel had recovered from its Babylonian conquest and returned to a ruined Jerusalem, the trauma of hopelessness overwhelmed them. This is where Israel's prophetic voices arise. God will provide another anointed figure (Messiah)—and God will send his Spirit to renew the land and its prospects. Isaiah 32 describes the devastation of conquest, then the prophet predicts a renewal that alone can come from God.

> The fortress will be abandoned,
> > the noisy city deserted;
> citadel and watchtower will become a wasteland forever,
> > the delight of donkeys, a pasture for flocks,
> till the Spirit is poured on us from on high,
> > and the desert becomes a fertile field,
> > and the fertile field seems like a forest.
> The LORD's justice will dwell in the desert,
> > his righteousness live in the fertile field.
> The fruit of that righteousness will be peace;
> > its effect will be quietness and confidence forever.
> > (Isaiah 32:14-17)

Isaiah is anticipating an utterly new era when the Spirit of God will renew everything and bring new hope to God's people. In some of the most poetically beautiful passages in all of the Bible, he shows that God is about to do a new thing.

> For I will pour water on the thirsty land,
> > and streams on the dry ground;

> I will pour out my Spirit on your offspring,
>   and my blessing on your descendants.
> They will spring up like grass in a meadow,
>   like poplar trees by flowing streams. (Isaiah 44:3-4)

Not only will God's Spirit begin the process of making a new creation, but the catalysts or agents of this renewing effort will also be uniquely anointed.

> Here is my servant, whom I uphold,
>   my chosen one in whom I delight;
> I will put my Spirit on him,
>   and he will bring justice to the nations. (Isaiah 42:1)

And again in Isaiah 61:1,

> The Spirit of the Sovereign LORD is on me,
>   because the LORD has anointed me
>   to proclaim good news to the poor.

It wasn't long before this expectation of an anointed person was fused to the expectation for the Messiah. Messiah means "anointed," so in the late Old Testament era, the hope for the Messiah and Spirit arose simultaneously.

But there is more. Not only would creation be renewed and the leader of this new world be anointed, but the citizens of this new creation would possess the Spirit in an unprecedented way. When the prophet Ezekiel imagines Israel returning from Babylon, the resumption of their life in Jerusalem is only a part of God's redemptive gift.

> For I will take you out of the nations; I will gather you from
> all the countries and bring you back into your own land.
> I will sprinkle clean water on you, and you will be clean; I
> will cleanse you from all your impurities and from all your

idols. I will give you a new heart and put a new spirit in you;
I will remove from you your heart of stone and give you a
heart of flesh. And I will put my Spirit in you and move you
to follow my decrees and be careful to keep my laws.
(Ezekiel 36:24-27)

In Ezekiel 37 the prophet famously imagines Israel as a valley of
dry bones. A cemetery. A place of death and defeat. But then
God promises a resurrection of Israel's national life: the emergence of new possibilities when skeletons take up new bodies
filled by God's Spirit. The same vision comes from Jeremiah (Jeremiah 31:31-34) and the prophets Zechariah (Zechariah 12:10)
and Joel (Joel 2:28-29). A new hope will be born in the land of
Israel when God opens a new chapter: peace will reign, righteousness will prevail, and God's anointed messenger will inaugurate a world of intimacy with God never before seen. And all
of this will be the work of God reaching into Israel's history
through his Spirit.

In the centuries immediately preceding the New Testament
(often called Rabbinic Judaism), the eschatological hope of Jeremiah and Ezekiel was almost extinguished. Little zeal for a
Spirit-transformed era was sought. It is common to read the
view that Haggai, Zechariah, and Malachi concluded the era of
the prophets and for the most part, the activity of the Spirit had
come to an end. This is reinforced by Jewish writings penned the
century before Jesus. What surfaces is that a commitment to
study and obedience was viewed as a gateway to righteousness.
And rather than talk of the Spirit, we find enormous emphasis
on the Torah. This term could refer to the Bible's first five books
or it could be used flexibly to describe all of the Hebrew Scriptures or, in some cases, the rabbinic commentary that accompanied them. But the idea is that the "Word of God" was the

locus of engagement with God, and Spirit encounters were rare. God, we might say, could be found in a holy book.

Understanding the New Testament's portrayal of the Spirit requires us to review this background simply because without it we cannot understand Israel's expectations in the centuries preceding the New Testament. The original hope portrayed an era of expectation and fulfillment, and as each generation passed, many thought that this era would dawn in their own time. It is truly a drama awaiting its final scene. This is attested as well by the many Jewish writings that fill in the picture after the Old Testament closes.

JESUS AND THE SPIRIT

To be concise, the New Testament is saying that the wait is over. The longed-for expectation of the postexilic period has now been fulfilled. Or, as Paul writes, "the culmination of the ages has come" (1 Corinthians 10:11). *The messianic era has arrived* (see chap. 2). This means that the time of the Spirit is upon Israel. The opening chapters of the four Gospels show that something new is afoot. A quick glance at Matthew's and Luke's nativity stories hint at this clearly: the Spirit is now active and preparing the way for the Messiah's birth and public appearing. In Luke 1–2 the Gospel refers to the Spirit no fewer than ten times.

The importance of John the Baptist in the gospel story is not merely that he identifies and baptizes Jesus, but that he is viewed as a prophet, akin to an Old Testament prophet (Matthew 11:9-15; Mark 11:32). He dresses like Elijah and evokes memories of the classic days of Old Testament history when God anointed prophets with his Spirit. But at the center of his work is his announcement of the coming Messiah. When Jesus arrives, his appearing is hallmarked by his baptism in the Jordan River. Here Jesus' identity is made plain, God's voice confirms his divine commission ("This is my beloved son"), and the Spirit rests on him. This is a signal of Jesus' identity as the anointed messenger from God, in this case, God's Son. For John's Gospel, this event is underscored: the Spirit not only descends on Jesus but it *remains* on him (John 1:33). This was no temporary anointing for office but something permanent that would be a feature of Jesus' ongoing efforts. His ministry would be a baptizing ministry as well—but not with water (John 4:2). Jesus would be a distributor (baptizer) of the Holy Spirit (John 1:33).

In John 3:34-35 John describes Jesus' ministry with these peculiar words: "For the one whom God has sent speaks the words of God, for [God] gives the Spirit without limit. The Father loves the Son and has placed everything in his hands." In the original language the bracketed word *God* does not appear ("for *he* gives the Spirit without limit"), and interpreters debate whether this describes God giving the Spirit to Jesus or Jesus giving the Spirit to us. But most are in agreement that this describes the endowment God has given Jesus, just as John 3:35 talks about the Father loving the Son and *giving all things* to him. Jesus has the Spirit of God on him in an unprecedented way.

The general picture is that Jesus *as Messiah* is the bearer of God's long-awaited Spirit in the world. It is a power that has almost a controlling presence in his life. After Jesus' baptism Mark says that "the Spirit immediately drove him out into the wilderness" (Mark 1:12 RSV). When Jesus delivers a person from demonic possession, it is the power of the Spirit that makes his effort effectual. In one important episode, Jesus is challenged by his opponents, who claim that he is working under the power of Satan. Jesus argues that if this is true, then Satan is defeating himself. He continues, "But if it is by the Spirit of God that I drive out demons, then the kingdom of God has come upon you" (Matthew 12:28). Here we have a combination of key terms:

messiah, Spirit, and kingdom. Jesus is offering to Israel the future that it awaited. The kingdom has arrived—the Messiah is here, and the Spirit is now at work in Galilee. According to Jesus, to misrepresent this truth and to attribute these powers to Satan is the severest sort of blasphemy (Matthew 12:31-32).

Jesus' self-awareness of the Spirit in his life is seen during his inaugural sermon, given in Nazareth (Luke 4:16-30). Here in the presence of old family friends, Jesus is invited to read from the Scriptures. He asks for the Isaiah scroll and locates Isaiah 61, perhaps one of the most famous messianic texts in the Bible. He then creates a patchwork with lines from Isaiah 61, 58, and 42.

> The Spirit of the Lord is on me,   [Isaiah 61]
>   because he has anointed me   [Isaiah 61]
>   to proclaim good news to the poor.   [Isaiah 58]
> He has sent me to proclaim freedom for the prisoners
>   [Isaiah 61]
>   and recovery of sight for the blind, [Isaiah 42]
> to set the oppressed free, [Isaiah 58]
>   to proclaim the year of the Lord's favor. [Isaiah 61]

The announcement is carefully crafted and unmistakable, which is why everyone stares at him in silence (Luke 4:20). Jesus then says that this text is now fulfilled (Luke 4:21). The word *anointed* here is the term for Messiah, but it is explained in terms of the Spirit. "The Spirit of the Lord is upon me." We have to rethink the significance of a statement such as this and apply it to the Old Testament framework outlined above. Jesus is the bearer of the promised Spirit, and this signals the dawning of the messianic age.

In another episode, Jesus was at a water festival during the Jewish Feast of Tabernacles. This took place in the autumn, when drought was particularly worrisome. During the dramatic water ceremony, where gallons of water were poured over the altar (as a form of prayer request to God), Jesus steps forward:

> On the last and greatest day of the festival,
> Jesus stood and said in a loud voice,
> "Let anyone who is thirsty come to me
> and anyone who believes in me drink.
> As the Scripture has said,
> rivers of living water will flow from his heart/belly
>   [Gk. *koilia*]."
>
> By this he meant the Spirit, whom those who believed in him were later to receive. Up to that time the Spirit had not been given, since Jesus had not yet been glorified. (John 7:37-39, author's translation)

Scholars have debated the punctuation of these verses for decades, and many today see the text as it is printed here. Believers are not the source of living water (or the Spirit), but Jesus is. He is the living water sought by Israel—the very image given in the promises of Jeremiah (Jeremiah 2:13; 17:13). He is the bearer of the Spirit into the world. John continues this imagery when Jesus comes to the cross. These waters will flow from Jesus' *koilia*. This may refer to the heart but only generally (the proper term for heart is *kardia*). *Koilia* is a person's stomach or abdomen. The soldier who pierces Jesus when he is on the cross with his lance does so at this location. At that moment water flows from Jesus' side (John 19:34). This image presents a series of vital ideas. Jesus is the bearer of the Spirit and when he dies, when his life is broken violently, the Spirit is symbolically released to the world.

This connection between the death of Jesus and the giving of the Spirit appears in Jesus' last words in the upper room. Five times Jesus promises that the Holy Spirit will be given to his disciples (John 14:16, 26; 15:26; 16:7, 13), but he clarifies that this gift of the Spirit is contingent on his departure or death: "It is for your good that I am going away. Unless I go away, the Advocate [or Spirit] will not come to you; but if I go, I will send him to you" (John 16:7). This explains why on the cross we see symbols of the Spirit's release. Living water flows from Jesus' body on the cross and, ironically, he is thirsty (John 19:28). And when Jesus dies, John describes it oddly: "After he bowed his head, he gave over the Spirit" (John 19:30, author's translation). This too is remarkable. While Matthew, Mark, and Luke use the conventional language of death for Jesus, John does not. Here we have the image that as Jesus passes from this world, something is happening: a gift is beginning to be unwrapped, and the Spirit is moving into the world. When Jesus meets them on Easter in a secluded room, the imagery continues when he breathes on them and says, "Receive the Holy Spirit" (John 20:22).

This detour into one detail of Jesus' life has been important in one respect. The New Testament is saying that in the arrival of the Messiah Jesus, the promised Spirit of God was ushered into the world. The Spirit was the power that animated Jesus' ministry, and it was a presence that would soon be given to the world upon his death. Luke knows this well. In some of Jesus' final words, he tells his disciples, "I am going to send you what my Father has promised; but stay in the city [of Jerusalem] until you have been clothed with power from on high" (Luke 24:49). The departure of Jesus carried with it the promise of the Spirit. This explains why Christians would ultimately see their allegiance to Jesus as including a necessary experience with the Holy Spirit.

THE EARLY CHRISTIAN EXPERIENCE

A major turning point in early Christian history took place fifty days after the Passover of Jesus' death. The resurrected Jesus had spent many days with his followers explaining his identity and mission, and after his ascension (Acts 1:9) the disciples remained in Jerusalem as Jesus had instructed. Jesus had promised that they would "receive power" when the Holy Spirit came upon them (Acts 1:8). When the Jewish festival of Pentecost arrived, the apostles and about 120 disciples were in Jerusalem, gathered together in one location. A strong wind began blowing, small flames of fire descended on them, and they were filled with the Spirit (Acts 2:1-4). These images are not incidental. Wind (as we now know) is a metaphor for the Spirit throughout the Hebrew Scriptures. Fire represented the presence of God, just as it did from the wilderness wanderings to the temple and its lampstand. In other words, the power of God—what we would expect at the temple—now had settled on the company of Jerusalem Christians. What one thought about the temple, one could think about the church.

This is when Peter gives the first public speech in the church's history explaining what has just transpired. This speech is enormously significant, for in it, Peter sets these events of Pentecost within the context of Israel's history. Peter cites the prophet Joel at length in order to convince his audience that this outpouring of the Spirit is not only what the Hebrew prophets predicted, but it is tied to Jesus' ongoing work to transform the world.

What is clear from the narrative in Acts is that conversion to Christ is linked to a profound experience of the Spirit. Not only is the audience at Pentecost invited to join this experience, but again and again as the church embarks on a new threshold of ministry (from Judea to Samaria to Gentile Caesarea) God confirms this missional step with yet another anointing of the Spirit (Acts 2:4; 8:17; 10:44; 11:15). When Saul (Paul) is converted, he likewise encounters the power of God when Jesus appears to him. When Paul met twelve new disciples near Ephesus, he inquired whether they had "received the Holy Spirit" when they believed. They had not and thus they were an anomaly. They had believed in Jesus and had been baptized, but there remained another element in their discipleship that was lacking. When Paul prayed and laid hands on them, they received the Spirit and began manifesting unique spiritual gifts.

Each of these stories from Acts—when seen as a template for discipleship—provides the same theme. *Belief in Jesus, baptism in Jesus' name, and receiving the Spirit were each constituent parts of what it meant to be a follower of Jesus.*

The centrality of the Spirit in Christian life and experience is reinforced throughout the New Testament. Paul is even willing to say that someone who does not have the Spirit within their life cannot belong to Christ (Romans 8:9)! When the apostle John writes letters to fledgling churches, he wants to give them tests that will determine whether they are part of Christ's true community. And again, it is the Spirit within someone's life that determines this. "This is how we know that we live in him and he in us: He has given us of his Spirit" (1 John 4:13).

This was the consistent pattern of life with the early Christian church. Your identity was not exclusively anchored to what you believed intellectually about Jesus (though this was important). It was also anchored to a dynamic experience of God that could be quantified only with difficulty. As in Nicodemus's conversation with Jesus (John 3), the Spirit is like the wind, which blows unpredictably. No one doubts its reality, but no one can calculate its movements.

The Spirit and the Church

Throughout the New Testament we see three features of the Spirit's work within the lives of Christians and the church. It is not as if the Spirit is an ambiguous form of inspiration that simply helps disciples succeed in life. The Spirit brings outcomes that have important consequences.

First, the Spirit sustains the life of Jesus within our lives. In his great farewell (John 13–17) Jesus promised that he would not leave us as orphans (John 14:18). That is, in his departure he would not abandon those he loves. Therefore his aim for his disciples is to create an interior life of intimacy and love that will sustain us for the duration of our lives. In John's Gospel Jesus delicately teaches a symmetry of intimacy that mimics his relation with the Father. As the Father loves and indwells the Son, so too the Son loves and indwells his disciples. And the means of this indwelling is the Holy Spirit. Thus Jesus can say, "Anyone who loves me will obey my teaching. My Father will love them, and we will come to them and make our home with them" (John 14:23). The many promises of the Spirit are given for reassurance so that we can know that Christ is dwelling in us. It is no surprise, then, that on Easter Sunday when Jesus appears and begins pouring his Spirit into them that he "breathed on them" (John 20:22), illustrating richly that *his Spirit* is available to them. As John will later write, "This is how we know that we live in him and he in us: He has given us of *his Spirit*" (1 John 4:13).

This also is the language of Paul in Romans 8:9: "If anyone does not have *the Spirit of Christ*, they do not belong to Christ." This is not just any Spirit; it is the Spirit that pours from Jesus himself. In a telling narrative in Acts 16, we find a truly amazing description of disciples who were trying to discern what choices were best as they moved forward:

> Paul and his companions traveled throughout the region of Phrygia and Galatia, having been kept by *the Holy Spirit* from preaching the word in the province of Asia. When they came to the border of Mysia, they tried to enter

Bithynia, but *the Spirit of Jesus* would not allow them to. So they passed by Mysia and went down to Troas. (Acts 16:6-8)

Note carefully Luke's language: the Holy Spirit prevented them from entering Asia, and the Spirit of Jesus prevented them from entering Bithynia. It is the spiritual presence of Jesus, the resurrected, ascended Jesus, who now accompanied them through the Holy Spirit.

Second, the New Testament Christians understood that one important outcome of the Spirit's work was the development of gifts in the church. We see references to these gifts of the Spirit in Romans 12:3-9 and Ephesians 4:1-16. Men and women were aware that their role in the church depended on discovering and using gifts not of natural talent but that were divinely given. The premier discussion of these gifts is in 1 Corinthians 12–14. In these chapters Paul contends with Christians who are promoting ecstatic speech gifts such as speaking in tongues and claiming that they are the greatest gifts that every believer should possess. This leads Paul to provide an outline of how a variety of gifts orchestrate the life and work of the church (1 Corinthians 12), why love should be the ultimate test of any gift (1 Corinthians 13), and how dramatic gifts such as prophecy and tongues should be tested inside the church (1 Corinthians 14).

These ideas give us a complex though unified picture of Christian life. The church in the New Testament is called the body of Christ (1 Corinthians 12:27), which means not simply that the church belongs to Christ but that he indwells the church and gives the church its life. His Spirit indwells its members and equips them to sustain Jesus' work so that it is not a cliché when we say that we are Jesus' hands and feet in the world. We sustain the efforts of Jesus inasmuch as we bear Jesus' Spirit and live within his community.

Third, the New Testament understands that the work of the Spirit brings about the moral transformation of Christ's people. When we think about Paul's teaching on the Spirit, we too often turn to 1 Corinthians, where he is actually brokering a sharp disagreement in Corinth about the Spirit. But Paul's most important discussion is likely in Romans 8, where we find more references to the Spirit than any other chapter. For Paul, the most profound problem within human life is its loss of the glory and righteousness God had intended from the beginning of creation. Paul sees the entry of the Spirit into our lives as giving us the power to overcome the sin that has devastated God's creation. "The mind governed by the flesh is death, but the mind governed by the Spirit is life and peace" (Romans 8:6). Paul is not framing a choice between dwelling on our sinful inclinations (flesh) and dwelling on our inner spirit (our better selves). Paul wants us to turn toward God's Spirit, who can empower and transform us. Years later Paul can describe to his disciple Titus what the fullness of our salvation looks like: "But when the kindness and love of God our Savior appeared, he saved us, not because of righteous things we had done, but because of his mercy. He saved us through the washing of rebirth and renewal by the Holy Spirit" (Titus 3:4-5).

The Holy Spirit is an unmistakable feature of normal Christian life in the New Testament. The arrival and distribution of the Spirit first on Jesus and then on the gathered community of the church is central to the New Testament's announcement that a new era in biblical history has emerged in the world. The Spirit of God was key to God's people being empowered and transformed *so that* they could become the people Jeremiah and Ezekiel and Joel imagined they could become.

We could say that this is the completion of God's work of salvation: making us whole. I do not simply want justification, I want completion or restoration—sanctification—that can make me as God imagines me to be. Moreover, this is also about the transformation of the world. Unless our societies begin to experience the transformations that follow a transformed people, then we are to be most pitied. It is the Spirit intervening in our lives, making us new, that will bring hope to the story of the world. The kingdom of God, where it appears around us, only has value and potency when it is accompanied by the same power exhibited by Jesus, who inaugurated this kingdom. Following Jesus without an encounter with the Spirit makes us an anomaly no different than the disciples in Acts 19. We will have a truncated discipleship that is unable to truly represent the kingdom of God that should be growing in the world.

- seven -

COMPLETION

*Then I saw "a new heaven and a new earth," for the
first heaven and the first earth had passed away.*

REVELATION 21:1

The New Testament has a distinctive understanding of time.
There was a beginning (when God created the world), there
is a middle (when Israel and the church participate in God's efforts to reclaim his creation), and there will be an end (when all
efforts will cease and God himself will bring the human story to
completion). This idea of history is linear: there is a beginning
and there is an end.

It's not uncommon to find people who have a sense that history
will have a terminus or end. We may even live with a sense of
impending crisis or tragedy about the future—but this is not the
same thing. I regularly speak with students who look at environmental catastrophe, threats to the earth's biosphere, political corruption, or wholesale human sinfulness (seen in things such as
poverty, human trafficking, or war) and believe strongly that our
time on earth either is nearly over or should be over.

In Chicago's famed Field Museum of Natural History, you can
explore the $17 million exhibit called *The Evolving Planet.* Here

in 27,000 square feet you can walk through 4.6 billion years of the earth's history illustrated in state-of-the-art displays. You can trace the "five great extinctions" that changed the planet. And you will learn that most extinctions destroyed about 70 percent of all species on earth (the third, the Permian–Triassic Extinction, took out 90 to 96 percent of all species). And when you emerge from the exhibit, you have this sobering feeling that another extinction must be inevitable. In truth, the exhibit leads you right to this idea. We are doomed—in a thousand years or so, but still, we're doomed. There will be an end to history as we know it, and (for some) the earth will remove this troublesome hominoid species called *Homo sapiens* and begin to heal itself. For a disturbing read, try Elizabeth Kolbert's *The Sixth Extinction* (2014). She provides evidence that the sixth extinction is underway right now. Or try Brooke Jarvis's *New York Times Magazine* article "The Insect Apocalypse Is Here" (November 27, 2018). Either of these will keep you up at night wondering how many years we have left.

The idea that there will be or ought to be an end to history rises repeatedly in Western thought, particularly in times of duress due to war, famine, or plague. Whenever we begin to think about these ultimate or climactic consequences for history, we are forming what theologians call an *eschatology*. This simply means a study of the "end," "final," or "ultimate" things (Gk. *eschaton*). Therefore, a thoughtful visitor to *The Evolving Planet* exhibit in Chicago would recognize that we are reading a "secular eschatology" that puts humanity on notice that its time as a species in not permanent.

The New Testament (as well as the Old Testament) is forward looking in the sense that it also has an anticipatory view of time. It has an eschatology. It looks forward to an era when something will happen that will change everything. In this case, the Bible looks to a time when God intervenes powerfully and climactically, when the curtain will be drawn on human history and creation is set right as it was intended in the beginning. It is not a view (as above) of earth exhausting itself or nature finding revenge or even humans destroying their own environment and experiencing the consequences of their foolishness. It is about God's intervention, judgment, and restoration of all things. It is about God reclaiming what is his.

THE OLD TESTAMENT AND THE END

The key phrase to describe this divine intervention in the Hebrew Bible is the *Day of the Lord.* Generally, it refers to God's intervention in Israel's history to bring about some resolution. The prophet Zephaniah thus describes the calamities brought about by the Assyrian conquest of the eighth century BC as the climactic day of God's judgment (Zephaniah 1:7, 14). The idea is that God acts decisively in history to achieve what he desires. The prophets used similar language during and after the Babylonian conquest in the sixth century BC.

But this notion that God would intervene, judge, and set things right was soon projected onto the distant future by the Hebrew prophets. One day God's will would be imposed on the world through a climactic intervention beyond all imagining. The final book of the Old Testament lays this out clearly. In Malachi 4 "the day" is coming when the evildoers of the world will be judged and God's righteousness will at last have free and unfettered rein. Isaiah imagines nature being restored so that wolves will dwell with lambs, leopards will live with goats, and children will have no fear of snakes (Isaiah 11:6-8; 65:25). The law of God will be written on our hearts and righteousness will prevail (Jeremiah 31:31-34). It is as if history will come full circle: what began in the Garden of Eden will return to the Garden of Eden—a world of goodness, peace, and intimacy with God.

But in one sense we must be clear that this is not "the end" as museum doomsayers would have it. It is the end of the ruin we live in today—but it is actually the promise of a new beginning in which creation itself is restored. This is an entirely different matter. This is not about catastrophe (unless you are the object of God's judgment), nor is it about extinction. It is about the recovery that begins on the other side of judgment.

We have already learned that there were many elements in this expectation of the Old Testament and the Jewish teachers of Jesus' day. The Messiah would arrive, the line of David would be restored, the Spirit of God would be poured out—and this would climax with God himself appearing in the world. Isaiah writes,

> See, the LORD is coming out of his dwelling
> to punish the people of the earth for their sins.
> The earth will disclose the blood shed on it;
> the earth will conceal its slain no longer. (Isaiah 26:21)

Zechariah provides remarkable detail about this coming of "the day of the Lord," and he too says the climax will be the coming of God: "You will flee by my mountain valley, for it will extend to Azel. You will flee as you fled from the earthquake in the days of Uzziah king of Judah. Then the LORD my God will come, and all the holy ones with him" (Zechariah 14:5).

Malachi completes his description with signs that should be noted so that the end will not take anyone by surprise. "See, I will send the prophet Elijah to you before that great and dreadful day of the LORD comes" (Malachi 4:5). This final thought from the Old Testament delivers us to the doorstep of the New Testament. Just as John the Baptist evoked memories of Malachi's prophecy (looking like Elijah), the New Testament was saying that yes, the kingdom and the Messiah and the Spirit were now beginning to advance on history. The "end" is underway.

THE BEGINNING OF THE END

The audacious claim we find in the New Testament is that the great eschatological promises of the prophets are now being fulfilled. This is why Jesus says that the kingdom of God is *now appearing*. In his first letter, Peter makes this claim: "He [Jesus] was chosen before the creation of the world, but was revealed in these last [Gk. *eschatos*] times for your sake" (1 Peter 1:20). Here Peter is explaining that Jesus' appearance signaled that the end times had begun. John can plea with his followers, "Dear children, this is the last hour; and as you have heard that the antichrist is coming, even now many antichrists have come. This is how we know it is the last hour" (1 John 2:18). Likewise, Hebrews 1:2 says, "But in these last [Gk. *eschatos*] days he [God] has spoken to us by his Son, whom he appointed heir of all things, and through whom also he made the universe." Explaining how we should be warned by the calamities that befell the Israelites in the wilderness, Paul writes, "These things happened to them as examples and were written down as warnings for us, on whom the culmination [or end, Gk. *telos*] of the ages has come" (1 Corinthians 10:11). The end of the ages has come? This is truly audacious.

Think of it this way: the New Testament is saying that the night that has been ever so long now is nearly over. Why? Because the dawn can be seen in the eastern sky. It is faint and hazy but it is unmistakable. Dawn is coming—in fact, dawn is inevitable, and before long the sun in its full glory will break over the horizon and banish the darkness. The dawn locks in the promise of the morning's coming in the same way that the coming of Christ locks in the promise of God's restoration of all things.

Recall the diagrams we studied in chapter two. The New Testament shifts Jewish eschatology by proclaiming that the future has arrived in the present. The present order of the world has been put on notice, and God has begun his intervention that will restore things fully. As Jesus prayed, "Thy kingdom come, thy will be done *on earth as it is in heaven.*" While all of these things have not been fulfilled completely, John the Baptist and Jesus were the initial overtures of God that will shift history.

In the first diagram, Judaism viewed the world as having a singular moment [↓] of dramatic intervention.

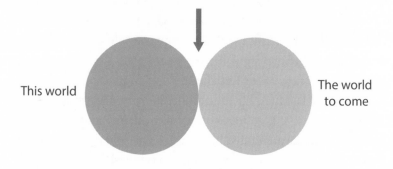

Figure 7.1

This singular shift in history predicted by the Hebrew prophets now has become the realization of what was promised only for the end of time. History has overlapped. God has entered the present age.

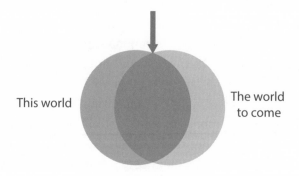

Figure 7.2

This means that an unprecedented reality has broken onto the world. The kingdom has come, and the great promises are being fulfilled. Or now we can say it another way: the end has begun to unfold itself with the coming of Jesus.

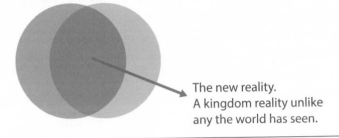

The new reality.
A kingdom reality unlike any the world has seen.

Figure 7.3

This is why the proper language to describe the arrival of Jesus and his kingdom is *eschatological.* We have in Christ something of the future now distributed in the world. To explain this Paul uses the helpful Jewish metaphor of "first fruits." First fruits were the initial offerings brought to the temple during the festival of Unleavened Bread (which followed right after Passover) and seven weeks later at the festival of Pentecost. After Passover a sheaf of barley was brought to the temple in recognition of the harvest now arriving. At Pentecost a wheat offering was similarly offered to God.

These were the first fruits that could be celebrated because more was on its way. Paul applies this image to Jesus, who in his resurrection is the "first fruits" from the dead (1 Corinthians 15:20, 23). He is the preliminary signal of what is yet to come and what is still to happen. Paul also refers to the Spirit as a "first fruit" because it too is an anticipatory gift of what is to come (Romans 8:23). God is even now showering the world with gifts that signal what creation will look like. And most astonishing, Christians are first fruits too because they now—in

their transformation by the Spirit into the likeness of Jesus—
reflect to the world what the goodness of the end of history will
look like (2 Thessalonians 2:13; James 1:18).

Therefore, we believe that the "beginning of the end" has come
upon us. The successes of Jesus' followers in the world do not
spring from an optimism about the progress of history. In fact it is
the opposite. The life of Jesus' followers is shaped by "first fruit"
gifts—harbingers from a different age, a future age. They announce
the promise of the ultimate restoration of all God's creation.

This means we have an orientation toward the end of all things
as we live today. Christian eschatology is mistaken if it simply
concentrates on prophecies of history's climax. Listen to Paul's
exhortation to the Christians in Rome:

> And do this, understanding the present time. The hour has
> already come for you to wake up from your slumber, be-
> cause our salvation is nearer now than when we first be-
> lieved. The night is nearly over; the day is almost here. So
> let us put aside the deeds of darkness and put on the armor
> of light. (Romans 13:11-12)

Paul is directing these Christians to order their lives rightly
because they should be living as if God's intervention that closes
history is nearly upon them. He gives the same advice to the
Corinthians (1 Corinthians 7:25-31) where he urges them to see
that "this world in its present form is passing away." He repeats
this for the Thessalonians (1 Thessalonians 5:1-11) where he famously echoes Jesus and says that the "day of the Lord" will
come as a thief in the night (1 Thessalonians 5:2; Matthew 24:36-
44). Peter sounds this theme as well when he writes, "Therefore,
with minds that are alert and fully sober, set your hope on the
grace to be brought to you when Jesus Christ is revealed at his
coming" (1 Peter 1:13; see also 1 Peter 4:7; 2 Peter 3:14). Christian

life therefore has an orientation toward the day of God's final resolution of history. When we experience the futility and discouragement of this world, we know that a greater victory is ahead. Even creation is longing for this victory when it too will be restored (Romans 8:19-22).

THE END OF THE END

But there will be an end to all things as we know them today. God's creation will not be destroyed, but the nature of common life as we know it will pass away. We could illustrate it as in figure 7.4.

This world

The world to come

Figure 7.4

Here we see that this world will come to an end, or better, our history as we know it will be completed and the reign of God will bring to creation all that God had envisioned in the beginning. In his letter to the Colossians, Paul offers a thorough profile of Jesus' identity and work. This is where Paul writes that Jesus is "the image of the invisible God, the firstborn over all creation" (Colossians 1:15; see Colossians 1:15-20). In this profile of the mission and work of Christ, Paul describes something unexpected: "For God was pleased to have all his fullness dwell in him [Jesus], and through him to reconcile to himself all things, whether things on earth or things in heaven, by making peace through his blood, shed on the cross" (Colossians 1:19-20). What is clear here is that the ultimate work of Christ is not simply his sin-absolving death on the cross, but the reconciliation of all creation to himself. Christ is God's agent over creation's restoration, and this will be accomplished when all things come to terms with his sovereignty.

In 1 Corinthians 15 we find the fullest description of Jesus' eschatological work for the world. After describing the death and resurrection of Jesus, Paul outlines the ongoing work of Jesus leading to the close of history. "Then the end will come, when he hands over the kingdom to God the Father after he has destroyed all dominion, authority and power. For he must reign until he has put all his enemies under his feet. The last enemy to be destroyed is death" (1 Corinthians 15:24-26). Here we have the exhaustive intervention of Christ, who on behalf of God overturns the systems of this world and imposes his own authority. *All things* must be subordinated to Christ's rule. And it is under this victory that creation will begin to flourish anew.

The New Testament does provide some details about this final intervention of God. But first it is clear that the date cannot be known (Matthew 24:36, 42; Mark 13:32-37). It also says that there are certain prerequisites that must be completed first (Matthew 24:14; 2 Thessalonians 2:2-8; 1 John 2:18). Nevertheless, we do not know ("You do not know when that time will come" [Mark 13:33]), and those who have speculated and been wrong have been ridiculed (2 Peter 3:4). But such confusion may be understandable. On some occasions end-time prophecies describe the destruction of Jerusalem in AD 70 (Mark 13) or the demise of Rome (Revelation). These are seen as evidence that God's judgment has already begun in the world even though they are not the final judgments of history. Still, the Gospels tell us that the church should be alert to signs that the end may be near. Here the parable of the fig tree (Mark 13:28-31) is perhaps the best picture of what we do.

Tender branches and new young leaves signal that summer is near; so too we should look for indications such as false teachers, public corruption, violence, wars, famine, natural disasters, antagonism against Christ, and the persecution of the church (2 Timothy 3:1-9; Matthew 24:6-7; Revelation 6:9-11). Satan will consolidate his opposition to God, and evil will reach new levels of horror. Those who oppose Christ are called "anti-Christs" generally (1 John 2:18-22; 4:3; 2 John 7), but the New Testament describes a figure whose role as "the Antichrist" or "man of lawlessness" is singularly oppressive and who uses religious deceit to manipulate the world (2 Thessalonians 2:3-12; Revelation 13:5-8).

JESUS RETURNS

The great climax of Christian eschatology is the return of Christ, which is announced throughout the New Testament (Matthew 16:27; Mark 8:38; 13:26; Acts 1:11; 1 Thessalonians 4:16; Hebrews 9:28; Revelation 19:11; etc.). The Old Testament language for this climax, "the day of the Lord" or "the day of God," is often appropriated from the Hebrew Bible to describe it (1 Thessalonians 5:2; 2 Thessalonians 2:2; Revelation 16:14). Sometimes it is called the "day of the Lord Jesus" or "the day of Christ" (1 Corinthians 1:8; 5:5; 2 Corinthians 1:14; Philippians 1:6, 10; 2:16). But we need to be clear: this is no minor teaching in the New Testament because it holds to the principle that Jesus is the catalyst for the consummation of history. He is God's representative, bringing order to creation and fulfilling the hopes of the Old Testament prophets. History will end, and God's rule will be established. And we will join him in this project. Jesus once said to his apostles, "Truly I tell you, at the renewal of all things, when the Son of Man sits on his glorious throne, you who have followed me will also sit on twelve thrones, judging the twelve tribes of Israel" (Matthew 19:28).

Jesus' return will not be a private affair for his followers alone. He will appear in power (Matthew 24:30), be seen by all (Matthew 24:27), destroy evil (Romans 16:20; 2 Thessalonians 2:8; Revelation 19:19-21), and judge the world (Matthew 25:31-33; James 5:9). But his vocation will also include the rescue and reward of those who have believed in him. He will call out to his people and gather them into a redeemed community (Matthew 24:31; 1 Corinthians 15:23; 1 Thessalonians 4:14-17; 2 Thessalonians 2:1), and this will include those believers who have died (1 Corinthians 15:23; 1 Thessalonians 4:16). In fact, we will all be changed in order to take on the new eschatological life enjoyed by Jesus (1 Corinthians 15:52). We will live with Christ and share his glory (Romans 8:18, 29; 1 Corinthians 15:49; Colossians 3:4).

The aim of all this activity is what Peter and John call a "new heaven and a new earth" (2 Peter 3:13; Revelation 21:1). But we need to read this—particularly the book of Revelation—carefully. It is not as if the present world will be displaced by another heavenly world, nor will this world be destroyed. As creatures we are tied to our creaturely lives here in the world. This is the realm that God had planned for us. He loves this world, and from the beginning he desired to have it be a reflection of his goodness and beauty. Therefore, this view is not (as many have said) re-demption *from the world*. It is about the redemption *of the world*.

ESCHATOLOGICAL TRAPS

This idea of the consummation of history, not as planetary self-destruction but as divine reclamation, is something that has brought enormous controversy over the centuries. Despite Jesus' explicit warnings that we will be surprised ("like a thief in the night") and that we do not know the hour, still, Christians have not resisted the temptation to study the "fig tree" (Mark 13:28), analyze signs of change, map the future, and make pronouncements.

Dubious and unscrupulous teachers and websites are widely known today, and they have made many thoughtful Christians cynical. In many mainline denominations eschatology is either dismissed or turned into a flexible metaphor. And among non-believers, such far-fetched teachings about the end of time have led to cynicism about the entire Christian faith.

I remember as a young Christian getting ahold of Hal Lindsey's little book *The Late Great Planet Earth* (1970). By 1990 almost thirty million copies had been sold. It was frightening as it outlined that *this generation* I was living in would see the end of the world. I once stood in the Valley of Armageddon in Israel in 1973 reading parts aloud and imagining blood as deep as horses' bridles. Flash forward: I also remember reading the book with advanced theology students in 2000 who examined every exegetical decision Lindsey had made. Together the class was shocked that anyone could interpret the Bible so recklessly and irresponsibly and that the Christian public would buy it. Today new books by "prophecy pastors" are doing the same thing, and their volumes line the shelves of Christian bookstores.

Divisions among Christians over marginal issues are likewise disappointing. Some readers may have already noticed themes I gingerly bypassed in the paragraphs above. For instance, some have taught that there will be a seven-year "tribulation" before Christ's second coming. This rests on virtually no biblical evidence—yet Christians believe it fervently. Others have taught that there will be a "rapture" of the church before this seven-year tribulation, and even less biblical teaching supports this idea. Indeed, the New Testament teaches that Christ's people will join him in the air (a "rapture," 1 Thessalonians 4:17), but this is linked to Christ's second coming (1 Thessalonians 4:16) when we, like Roman citizens, rush out of the city gates to welcome our returning hero from war.

Then there is Revelation 20:1-7 and the thousand-year reign of Christ (the millennium). Many Christians have chosen to see this as a literal period, while many others have viewed it as a metaphor within John's apocalyptic drama. Both are taking the text seriously. In fact, all of the book of Revelation beyond chapter three has led to controversy at some point. Is it a pictorial drama teaching one truth about God's victory? It is a detailed prophecy about the end of the world? Is it depicting the demise of secular powers and the end of time, or is it targeting the contest between God's people and the Roman Empire in the first century? Good Christians have held each of these views. Perhaps it is time for more humility and less hubris when we interpret this perplexing book.

A modern eschatological heresy that future generations will find incomprehensible has to do with the Middle East. For some Christians throughout the world, the return of the Jews to Israel in the twentieth century and the establishment of the state of Israel in 1948 served as a "marker" indicating the fulfillment of prophecy and the near-return of Christ. Therefore Christians are obligated to support and promote this divine event because it is God's end-time work in the Middle East. Which is why the modern state of Israel is the focal point of so much Christian speculation. This even has a name: Christian Zionism. It is deeply controversial, and many Christians don't just disagree about this, they become furious. Some of my friends shake their heads and think it has reached manic proportions in some churches. Being pro-Israel can seem as essential as being pro-Jesus.

This sort of teaching is filled with innumerable pitfalls. First, it lacks historical perspective because many Christians in times past have said the very same things about their era. "But this time it's different" is simply unpersuasive. A close study of

Christian eschatological fervor in the sixteenth century is a sobering exercise when we learn that such passions have been repeated century after century. Second, while it is a good and wonderful thing that Judaism has a place of refuge and safety in modern Israel, a *theological* commitment to Israel has led to a Christian endorsement of Israeli exceptionalism and privilege that has made the country exempt from ethical criticism. Third, orthodox Jews throughout Israel and the world recognize that Israel is a purely secular state and therefore they cannot see it serving God's purposes. Western Christians have trouble seeing this. A Jewish friend in Israel told me recently that American Christians are more passionate about Israel than Israelis. And it scares them. Perhaps then we need to take a step back because in many cases eschatology is swamping our ability to think critically. And fourth, whenever Christians tie their faith to specific political realities and call them fulfilled prophecies, their faith is at risk. Because when those political realities collapse, so does their faith. Again, Jesus said that we do not know when history will come to its end—we will be surprised—so we would do well to be wary of those who are quick to point out fulfilled prophecy.

We are not the first Christians to look at our world and be troubled—and wish for God's swift and decisive intervention. We may think that today's political turmoil, environmental crises, poverty, and violence are unparalleled. They are not. And again, it doesn't work to say, "But this time it's different." I wonder sometimes what Christians were feeling in the fourteenth century as the Black Death (or plague) swept through Europe and Asia, killing from 75 to 200 million people. By some estimates, one-third of Europe was wiped out. Or I've thought about Christians living in about 1916 in the middle of World War I, wondering how humanity could sink to such devastating and violent levels. About 12 million died. Each era deems its suffering to be the most profound and worthy of God's judgment.

Our comfort is knowing that God is not unaware of history. That he is guiding it purposefully to its conclusion. That judgment awaits the sinful either when they die or when they meet the returning Christ. That God is eager to take back his creation and he plans to do so. Hope in God's renewal of his world not only gives us confidence to go on living, but it can redeem our commitment to the world itself. In past generations, Christians have said that because our hope is outside this world, their own commitment to the world was diminished. The world becomes disposable and subject to misuse. But an eschatology that redeems creation, awaiting God's intervention to restore it—an eschatology that plants our future firmly inside creation itself—this eschatology has possibilities we may have never expected. We become buoyant and resilient as we live in this troubling world because we know that a better end-plan may unfold any day.

CONCLUSION

The aim of a study such as this is simple: it is to understand the great theological panorama of what God is doing in human history. That story will explain to us how we entered into the predicament we are in, how we might remedy it, and where we'll end up. We might even say that our *entire story* with God is eschatological because it is moving toward some climactic purpose. And if we understand the Bible well, we begin to understand the steps in that redemptive process (from creation, to corruption, to re-creation or transformation in Christ). God has not abandoned his creation. He is at work saving it from creatures like us who have lost the glory that they were destined to possess. This theological panorama is a story, a complex story because we are complex people, but a story nevertheless about diminishment and restoration. If I had one heartfelt wish it would be that we would reclaim that story and see our Christian lives as a co-conspiracy with God in the redemption of this world. Because if we get that right, it will change how we live from day to day, how we arrange our priorities, how we vote, how we work, how we spend our money, and what we commit to. It will shift the mission of the church, which has so often preached a truncated version of this narrative and given us a little story instead of a big story.

Christians who have not understood the grand panorama of God's project in the world often reduce Christian life and faith to selective themes that are taken out of the project and set in isolation. So for some, the message of the gospel is accepting Christ, living a Christian life, and awaiting our salvation in heaven. The problem with this teaching isn't that it is wrong but that it is incomplete and tragically short-sighted. And it misrepresents the larger story that is filled with so many more riches. Some Christians will lift passages about the Holy Spirit from the New Testament and speak incessantly about how Spirit-experience is the main theme of Christian life. Others will reduce the gospel to social justice or dramatic teachings about the end of history. The problem is not any one of these is incorrect (unless they are handled poorly) but that they lack context and complexity. They only promote the part because they do not understand the whole.

I recently visited the Denver Art Museum's exhibit *Rembrandt as Painter and Print Maker* (2018). This is a marvelous collection that is currently appearing in select US cities. It contains rarely viewed Rembrandt prints collected from all over the world. I

Figure 8.1. Close-up of the face of Jesus from Rembrandt's *Hundred Guilder Print*

stood in front of the famous *Hundred Guilder Print* of Christ, who is portrayed preaching to a large audience. Rembrandt made this engraving in 1648, and it belongs to the Bibliothèque Nationale de France in Paris. But here I was, inches from the real thing. I had seen reprints of the close-up portrait of Jesus' face from this piece many times. I had seen it printed alone on covers of books. *But no one told me that it belonged to one of the most fantastic 17th century art engravings in the world.* I remember standing still, catching my breath, silenced, and seeing what I had not seen before. This was not just about Jesus' face. I saw the larger panorama of Rembrandt's project and realized that while Jesus' portrait was stunning and beautiful, still, the crowds who were surrounding him were also the artist's subjects. This was the world in all its misery and sin and presumption, and in its midst was a radiant Christ (light beaming from his face), who with outstretched arms was coaxing these people to see a better way.

Figure 8.2. Rembrandt's *Hundred Guilder Print*

When we study the New Testament and weave together the themes that are presented in this book—fulfillment, kingdom, cross, grace, covenant, spirit, and completion—we weave together a tapestry that is at once complex and beautiful. And for the first time we see the whole just as I saw the whole of Rembrandt's real intentions. It takes extra work to comprehend the larger panorama of God's project for history, but it is worth it because it makes our faith thoughtful and nuanced and flexible. Suddenly the right things take priority, eccentric teachings are checked, and primary teachings are elevated.

In a word, we become mature. And that maturity, anchored to deep understandings of God's program and rich experiences with God's presence in our lives, makes us capable to address things we have not thought about addressing before. A student once came to me and asked me what the Bible said about protecting the environment. She was looking for "the right verse" that she could take with her for future reference. I didn't supply it. But I wanted her to understand creation and God's aims in a manner that her concern about the environment would take care of itself. *She needed the whole but she came seeking the part.* I've had people ask me about a myriad of themes, and they were doing this same thing. What one verse cinches the argument about gender or sexual orientation or abortion or the Middle East? The Bible has plenty to say about these, but they are embedded in a rich theological program, and those who take the time to study that program will come away capable to answer these and a host of new unanticipated questions they never imagined they could answer before.

My own prayer is that this study—and the other studies that will join this short book—will be used in the church to enrich and strengthen. I began by writing about my church's midweek program. This is my hope for where we go next: Imagine if church members (just like we do in classes) read these books as homework and they were linked to a series of sermons that reinforced the key themes. Imagine how we could deepen our understanding of the New Testament, the Old Testament, and other subjects not for the sake of mere education, but to help the body of Christ become well-equipped, resilient, and wise in how we live into God's efforts in the world.

DISCUSSION QUESTIONS

CHAPTER 1: FULFILLMENT

1. When the Gospels introduce Jesus to their readers, what do they want us to understand about Jesus' impact on the great story of the Old Testament?

2. How was Israel "still in exile" during the period of Jesus' life? How was Jewish hope framed in this period?

3. What was the basic idea of the Messiah, and how did Jesus fulfill it?

4. What claim do the Gospels make about Jesus that goes far beyond what Judaism was thinking? In other words, what was Jesus' unexpected relationship to God?

5. Is it enough to say that Jesus was an inspiring first-century teacher whom we ought to follow?

CHAPTER 2: KINGDOM

1. What was Jesus' primary project for the world? What did he want to accomplish?

2. What would an average Roman ruler think when he heard Jesus' language about "kingdom"?

3. How did Judaism understand God's "kingdom rule" to be available in the present and in the future?

4. How does Jesus utterly upend these Jewish expectations?

5. Where do we see Jesus' kingdom today? What wrong ideas have been taught? And how can we promote this kingdom correctly?

CHAPTER 3: CROSS

1. Why are Christians today immune to the drama of the cross?

2. Why were Jesus' audiences ill-prepared to recognize the necessity of the Messiah dying?

3. Does Jesus die as a martyr for his cause? Did his arrest and violent death take him by surprise?

4. When John the Baptist introduces Jesus as "the lamb of God who takes away the sins of the world" (John 1:29), what is the fullest meaning of his words?

5. How can the cross "reappear" in the church today as a central idea and symbol for who we are?

CHAPTER 4: GRACE

1. Do you agree that we've become immune to hearing the word *grace* as a major spiritual concept?

2. How can we see the basic idea of grace at work in the Old Testament story of Abraham? What about Moses and the Israelite departure from Egypt?

3. If grace is such a central idea to the New Testament, how does Jesus demonstrate it in his deeds and in his teachings?

4. Why was grace so fundamental to Paul's life experience and his teaching? Why did he feel he needed to defend it so firmly?

5. If we measure our lives through performance, achievement, and competition—why do we have such a hard time experiencing grace?

CHAPTER 5: COVENANT

1. If ancient life was lived corporately (in a tightly knit group), do you agree that modern life is lived promoting individualism?

What effect has this had on your Christian identity and the church?

2. How is Abraham so central to "covenant thinking" in the Old Testament?

3. Why does the New Testament refer to Abraham so many times? What is this saying about the Christian covenant community and its relationship to Old Testament Israel?

4. Why does Paul want to say—or how can Paul even say—that a Gentile can be a "child of Abraham"? Why is this important?

5. If the church is linked to Abraham, then what is the nature of the church's privileges, identity, and duties in the world? Does this affect how we read the Old Testament?

CHAPTER 6: SPIRIT

1. How does the Holy Spirit fit into the wider redemptive program of God for creation?

2. The Spirit appears with frequency in the Old Testament. But how was the Spirit's work limited? And what did the prophets anticipate as they looked forward to a new era?

3. How do the Gospels tell us that "the era of the Spirit" has arrived?

4. Did the early church believe that Spirit-experience was essential (or required) for being a true follower of Jesus? Think about the book of Acts or Paul's teaching.

5. What is measurable evidence that a person (as Paul wrote in Romans 8:9) "has the Spirit of Christ"? What makes you uncomfortable about all of this? What makes you hopeful?

Chapter 7: Completion

1. Do you believe that the world today is giving us an "eschatology"? Is this leading us to despair or to hope?

2. If God has built history with a terminus, what does the Bible say his purposes will be at "the end" of all things?

3. Can you explain how the New Testament shifts the eschatology of the Old Testament? How can we say that the beginning of the end has arrived?

4. What are some of the "traps" we need to avoid today when popular teachers begin to interpret modern history (in the Middle East) or emphasize environmental catastrophes?

5. When you think of the end of history, judgment, and the second coming of Christ, does it fill you with anxiety or hope? Why?

NOTES

INTRODUCTION

[1]This is Willow Creek Community Church in Chicago's western suburbs, one of the largest churches in America. Wednesday evenings at 7:00 p.m. a "Midweek Gathering" brings together about 1,000 people for 25 minutes of worship and almost 40 minutes of teaching. These people are the core of Willow—men and women who want more, who are studying the Scriptures with intentionality, and who take their faith very seriously.

Despite Willow's difficult and painful journey in 2018, it remains a remarkable and vibrant place. Today's new leadership is reshaping the church—a congregation populated with thousands of amazing Christians whose spiritual maturity and intentionality continue to inspire me.

1 FULFILLMENT

[1]Rabbi Jacob Neusner, *A Rabbi Talks with Jesus* (Montreal: McGill-Queen's University Press, 2000).

4 GRACE

[1]Some readers will know at once that I am following the South Galatians Theory. This theory argues that while ethnic or tribal Galatia was in the far north, a Roman redrawing of provincial boundaries formed a new province called imperial Galatia as far south as the Taurus mountains. By this reckoning, when Paul was on his first tour he was in imperial Galatia. New inscriptional evidence has now made this case fully convincing.

SCRIPTURE INDEX